beautiful botanicals

45 APPLIQUÉ FLOWERS & 14 QUILT PROJECTS

deborah kemball

C&T PUBLISHING

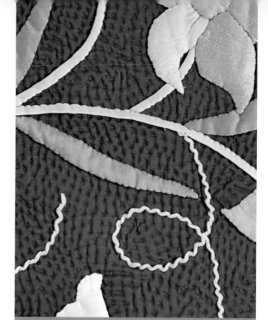

Published by C&T Publishing, Inc., P.O. Box 1456, Lafayette, CA 94549

Library of Congress Cataloging-in-Publication Data

Kemball, Deborah.

Beautiful botanicals : 45 appliqué flowers & 14 quilt projects / Deborah Kemball.

p. cm.

ISBN 978-1-57120-961-0 (soft cover)

1. Appliqué--Patterns. 2. Quilting--Patterns. 3. Flowers in art. I. Title.

TT779.K46 2011

746.44'5--dc22

2010021402

Printed in China

10 9 8 7 6 5 4 3 2 1

Dedication

For Benj, Nick, Hugo, Max, and Gus, with my love

Acknowledgments

Thanks to Den Haan & Wagenmakers BV in Amsterdam for their kind donations of great quantities of gorgeous red tone-on-tone chintz.

CONTENTS

PREFACE

Like many other quilters, I trod a fairly intensive path of embroidery, knitting, and tapestry before discovering quilting. While living in Eindhoven in the south of the Netherlands and being heavily pregnant with our third son, I passed a quilt shop and was awed by the baby quilt in the window. Intrigued, I went in and was dazzled by the huge array of fabrics and quilts on display. I left with a large bag of fat quarters and instructions for my first quilt. The die was cast. I dropped my knitting needles, tapestry needles, and everything else and became addicted to fabric and quilts.

After our time in the Netherlands, my husband's work took us to Costa Rica, where I found a treasure trove of discount fabric shops selling quilting fabric from the United States. Nearly all the fabric was flawed in some way or other, so I could buy yards of fabric for cents at a time. Liberated by the cheap prices, I became an enthusiastic machine piecer, averaging one newly made quilt every three weeks. But my machine, hammering away through triangles and squares, added the agony and frustration of mismatched seams and made me tense and dissatisfied. I decided that perhaps I wasn't cut out for machine piecing and quilting; as a result, I became very keen on hand quilting. I made a number of self-designed white-on-white wholecloth quilts and strippies that remain some of my favorites to this day. Their Spartan white simplicity worked well in the tropics where, with so much riotous color of flowering trees, bougainvillea, and hibiscus going on outside our windows, we preferred simple cool interiors.

By this time, I was beginning to consider appliqué. Several years earlier, I had made five small appliqué blocks, which I had designed myself. These blocks were heavily influenced by my previous designs for tapestries and were quite unlike any traditional appliqué normally associated with quilting. I decided that during our move to Canada, when I foresaw long periods in small hotel rooms, I would make a hand-appliquéd Baltimore Album–style quilt. I looked at pictures of Baltimore quilts online; however, though I could appreciate the huge amount of work that had gone into all of them, I found their designs very busy. So instead, I decided to alternate the wreaths and hearts with individual flowers.

Completely by accident, when playing around with the individual flower designs in my Baltimore Album quilt, I became fascinated with the new patterns made by repeating the flower along various axes of symmetry. I decided to bring these designs into the quilt too. By the time I had completed the quilt, I knew that in appliqué I had found my real love in the world of quilting.

I discovered that I could transpose my flower design ideas well within this medium. Less influenced by traditional appliqué design and more by the chintzes of the eighteenth century, I experimented with moving outside the traditional block concept by using swirling floral designs and borders.

I had my big color renaissance during our first Quebec winter. Our white quilts and white sofas looked so bleak against the endless winter landscape, which marks Quebec for nearly half the year. Until then, I had only lived in the tropics and in Europe, so I had never realized how much I needed color until it was absent for so long. I began working with bright reds and loved the results and the joy of combining colors.

I have really found what I love to do. It has also been an unexpected pleasure to see my patterns created in such a wide variety of fabrics by students who put their own ideas into my designs.

I hope that you enjoy all of these designs and that you will put yourself and your own ideas into them, so they become unique and all the more special.

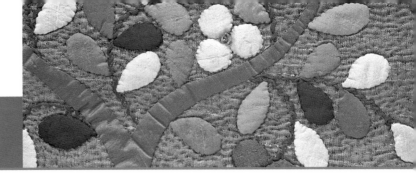

INTRODUCTION

I am known among my students for my belief that quilting can be achieved with minimal tools, in the same way that quilting was done centuries ago. I find I need very little in terms of special equipment. In fact, if you were to look at the mess of my sewing drawers, I don't think you would be able to guess that I am a full-time quilter. It's not an impressive collection.

You would find:

- standard scissors (which, contrary to the rule, I use for everything, paper included)
- a few odd pins
- Roxanne Between Needles No. 9 (which I use for absolutely all my sewing)
- a roll of freezer paper
- Mylar heatproof plastic
- a diverse selection of threads
- several cheap basic metal thimbles (which I wear until they wear through)

Thimble wearing is a good habit. I feel uneasy and cannot sew if I don't have one on the middle finger of my right hand when sewing or on both middle fingers when quilting.

Only my collection of threads might give away my love of appliqué. I sometimes use monofilament silk, but I confess that it makes me tense and bad tempered, because my heavy hand frequently breaks the thread. I am fast and ruthless with my needle. Although I prefer Gutermann coarser silk thread, I have found that their color choice is limited. I am not in the least bit averse to using whatever thread I can find in my drawers if the color works.

For marking fabric, the special fabric-marking pencils always seem to break. Instead, I tend to use my children's colored pencils in white or yellow.

I use standard white rubber erasers that I cut with scissors into fine points for hard-to-reach areas.

I use great spools of masking tape for everything, from hanging my designs on windows to cleaning off the loose threads that cling to me endlessly. I also use it to clean my ironing board at the end of each day.

My iron seems to be permanently on. I shock intrepid quilters by using it at very high heat—even pressing my silk quilts with a really hot, steaming iron.

I love Hobbs wool batting because it's like quilting through butter. I also like the loft it gives with my heavy echo quilting.

I have a fabric stash, but it is not as huge as one might expect. I love to use the tone-on-tone chintzes from Den Haan & Wagenmakers in Holland. I have several of their gorgeous floral fabrics for fussy cutting. In addition to those, I have a large selection of fat quarters in prints, batiks, and commercial hand dyes.

A cursory glance at the pictures in this book will give away the fact that I love red. I can't get away from it, nor do I want to. However, I can assure you that I have seen my designs made in every other color, and they look equally lovely in all the colors of the rainbow.

How to Use This Book

In Part 1: The Flowers (pages 12–51), you will find templates and detailed instructions for creating all the flowers. Although presented in sizes to fit 7˝ blocks, the flowers are actually intended purely as a reference for the projects in Part 2 (pages 52–99). The similar scale of the flowers means that they are all interchangeable and can be substituted for one another in the different projects. So if you particularly love one flower more than another, you can easily substitute it.

In addition to the large number of flowers, you will find five different border options in Part 3: The Borders (pages 100–105). I hope you will want to challenge yourself and combine the flowers and borders to your delight. The possibilities are almost limitless.

Palampore Tree of Life (page 109) shows how well one block can be surrounded by consecutive borders. If you aren't feeling very ambitious, a single bloom surrounded by the simplest border of all—the Simple 1˝ Sawtooth Border (page 100)—is a lovely project to get you started. Should you feel like a challenge, both *Floral Sampler* (page 85) and *Floral Fantasy* (page 94) use almost all the flowers shown in Part 1. I am delighted with these two quilts, both of which portray the look I love most of all—a mass of trailing stems and flowers. These two quilts are reminiscent of the gorgeous chintz designs that found their way from India to Europe in the eighteenth and nineteenth centuries and that remain, for me, designs of timeless beauty.

THE BASICS

Positioning Appliqués on the Background

NOTE

Although Option 1 is my preferred method, it requires that you photocopy and enlarge the reduced version of the pattern to a full-size pattern and trace it onto the background fabric. This method is used in the instructions presented throughout this book. For the larger quilts, I highly recommend that you follow this method.

If you prefer not to make a full-size pattern, however, you can follow Option 2 to position the appliqués and embroidery.

OPTION 1: TRANSFERRING THE PATTERN

1. Photocopy the design, enlarging it to full size , if necessary. Large designs can be copied in sections and taped together or taken to a photocopy shop and enlarged in one piece.

2. Use masking tape to attach a full-size paper pattern to a window. Tape the background fabric on top of the pattern. Make sure that the fabric edges are aligned properly before taping the top and bottom.

3. Trace the design onto the background fabric (I use a standard white colored pencil). Trace slightly inside the lines of the paper pattern motifs to avoid erasing colored pencil marks after appliqué.

TIP

When tracing, you don't have to mark every detail of the design; just mark enough to position the appliqués and stitch the embroidery. Mark the berries, grapes, and other template circles and ovals with a cross or dot.

OPTION 2: USING A DRAWING FOR PLACEMENT

Refer to the template as a guide. Start in the middle of the design and position the appliqués, using the pattern for reference. This method is easier to accomplish with small projects than with large ones.

Making Small Circles and Ovals

Many of my flowers are made with premade circles and ovals, using Mylar or cardstock templates. Use a largish seam allowance to make the berries and petals look stuffed and to add extra texture to the finished piece. Heavy echo quilting makes them pop out even more.

1. Use a fine permanent marker to trace the motif onto Mylar or cardstock.

2. Cut out the shapes on the line.

3. Place the template on the right side of the fabric and cut out the shape, leaving a ¼″ seam allowance.

TIP

For oval shapes, place the length of the template shape on the bias of the fabric, if possible. This makes it much easier to form smooth curves during appliqué.

4. Knot a piece of thread and make a small neat running stitch ⅛″ from the outer edge.

5. Place the template on the reverse side of the fabric.

Trace, cut out, and baste the shape.

6. Pull the thread to gather the fabric tightly around the template. Press with a hot iron.

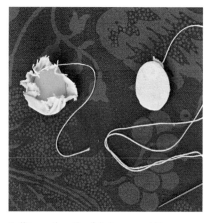

Pull to gather the fabric around the template.

7. When cool, remove the template, gather the fabric, and press again.

> ■ **TIP**
>
> *Leave a long thread so that you can regather the shape if it has lost its sharp creases.*

Using Freezer Paper Templates

Use freezer paper to make your templates (except the circle and oval shapes). I never leave my freezer paper on the fabric during appliqué.

1. Place freezer paper, shiny side down, onto the pattern to be copied. Trace the shape.

2. Cut out the shape on the line.

3. Use a hot, dry iron to press the freezer paper, shiny side down, onto the right side of the fabric. Whenever possible, place the length of the freezer paper shape on the bias of the fabric.

4. Cut out the shape, leaving a generous ¼″ seam allowance. Snip inner curves if necessary, as shown in the following photo. Curves will appliqué easier and curvier this way!

Press, cut out, and clip.

Embellishing

WHIPSTITCH

I use a whipped running stitch for stems, tendrils, and stamens extensively. This stitch produces a bold, wavy line, perfect for tendrils.

1. With embroidery floss, stitch a small running stitch on the marked line. I usually use all 6 strands for stems and tendrils and 3 strands for stamens and other embellishments.

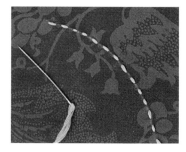

Stitch a small running stitch.

2. With the eye of the needle, weave the thread loosely back through each running stitch. (Using the eye of the needle instead of the point will prevent snagging the fabric.) Secure the thread on the wrong side of the background fabric.

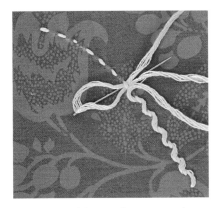

Use the eye of the needle to weave the thread through the stitches.

DETACHED BUTTONHOLE STITCH

This stitch works well for stamen heads.

1. Using all 6 strands of embroidery floss, make a ⅜″ stitch at the stamen end of the stem.

2. Make a second stitch in the same place as the first.

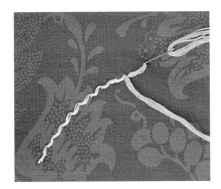

Make 2 stitches.

3. Bring the needle and thread to the top of the fabric. Make a loop around the double stitches, without going through the fabric.

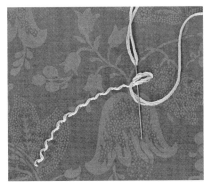

Loop thread around the stitches.

4. Pull the thread taut, so it makes a blanket-style stitch around the 2 threads.

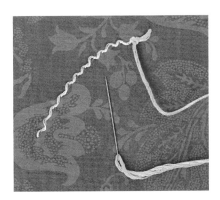

Pull the thread taut.

5. Repeat to make a second blanket stitch.

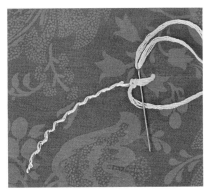

Make a second stitch.

6. Continue in this way until you have blanket stitched the entire length. Fasten off on the reverse of the fabric.

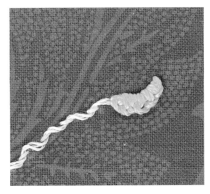

Finished stitch

BEADS

I love to use tiny beads, seed pearls, and crystals to embellish my flowers. I find the easiest needle to use is a No. 10 between, which will go through the tiniest of beads. I sew on embellishments after quilting and binding.

Appliquéing Stems

SINGLE-CURVE STEMS

I use the following quick-and-easy method to add bias stems.

1. Cut a ⅜″-wide bias strip.

2. Place the strip on the fabric, right sides together, with the upper edge of the bias against the inner curve of the marked stem line. Stitch about ⅛″ along the upper edge of the bias with a neat running stitch.

Place the bias strip and secure with a running stitch.

3. Finger-press the loose raw edge under to the stitch line. Then fold it over so the folded edge aligns with the pencil line.

4. Slipstitch the stem in place, covering the raw edge.

Fold the strip and slipstitch.

MULTIPLE-CURVE STEMS

Appliquéing single-curve stems only works if you slip-stitch along the outer curve. If you have a stem that waves in two or more directions, you must create each curve individually. Stitch curve A completely, rotate the work 180°, then stitch curve B, and so on.

1. Stitch curve A, following the instructions for appliquéing single-curve stems.

Stitch curve A.

2. Rotate the work 180°. Sew a running stitch for curve B, starting as close to curve A as possible.

Rotate 180° and stitch.

3. Finish curve B as you did curve A.

Finish curve B.

Appliquéing Leaves

Wavy-bottomed leaves are one of my favorite leaves, especially for daisies, peonies, and chrysanthemums.

Wavy-bottomed leaf

1. Cut out the leaves using freezer paper templates (page 8), leaving a ¼˝ seam allowance. Snip the fabric to the template along the inner curves.

Cut out the leaf and snip inner curves.

2. Remove the freezer paper template. Match the leaf to the pencil line and baste in place with 2 or 3 long stitches along the leaf's center to hold it in place. Turn under the edge and blindstitch along the leaf's upper edge, starting ½˝ from where the leaf will join the stem and stitching toward the stem.

Baste and stitch.

3. Turn under the leaf at the stem end and continue the blind stitch, finger-pressing and turning under as you go. Keep the stitches small and close together to prevent fraying along snipped inner curves.

Continue turning under and stitching.

4. Remove the basting and press well.

Remove basting and press.

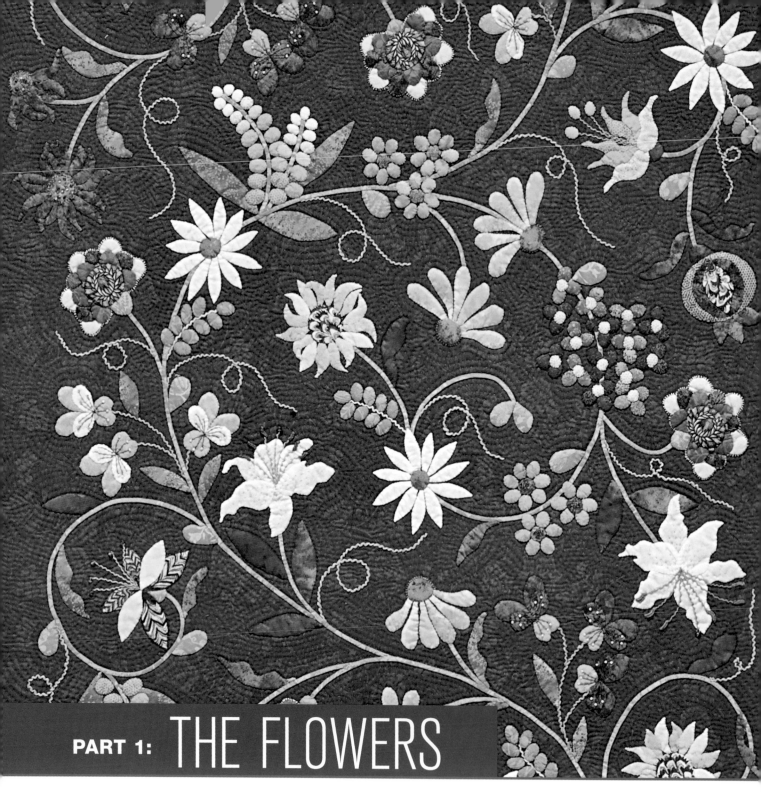

PART 1: THE FLOWERS

The flower patterns and instructions in this chapter will serve as a guide to creating all of the flowers included in the projects in Part 2 (pages 52–99). Although presented in sizes to fit 7″ blocks, they can be used either to make individual small projects or combined to make larger quilts. They can also be enlarged or reduced, as desired, for your original designs.

> **TIP**
>
> *Whenever possible, place your templates for leaves and petals on the bias of fabric. This makes it much easier to form smooth curves during appliqué.*

BALTIMORE BEAUTY FLOWER

I designed this flower years ago for my first appliqué project. Although it is more stylized than and quite different from my other flowers, I have kept it in my repertoire, as it has great potential in terms of fussy cutting and color. I often fussy cut the B piece if I can and then decide the colors of the flower according to this central piece.

Refer to pages 7–11 for general appliqué information.

1. Trace the design lines onto the background fabric.

2. Use Mylar templates to make petals A, B, and C. Use freezer paper templates to make petal D, petal E, and the lower leaf F. Make 2 C's and cut fabric in half to make 4 petals.

3. Cut a ⅜″-wide bias strip for the stem.

4. Appliqué the C petals and then the A piece. You will cover many of your drawn lines, but the base of the oval should sit in the base of the drawn flower.

> **NOTE**
>
> *You could remove the excess fabric of oval A before placing oval B, but I leave ovals intact. I like the added puffiness the thickness of the fabric adds to the texture.*

Prepare the appliqué pieces.

Appliqué the oval.

5. Add the stem. Keep the bottom of the oval on the base of the flower as you stitch oval B on top of oval A. Stitch on 2 E petals.

6. Cover with the D leaves. You will still have adequate drawn lines for correct placement.

7. Add the lower leaf F and embroider the tendril with a whipstitch (pages 8 and 9).

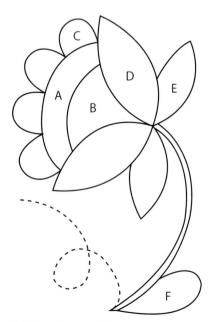

Complete the appliqué and add embroidery.

Baltimore Beauty Flower
Enlarge placement diagram 200%.

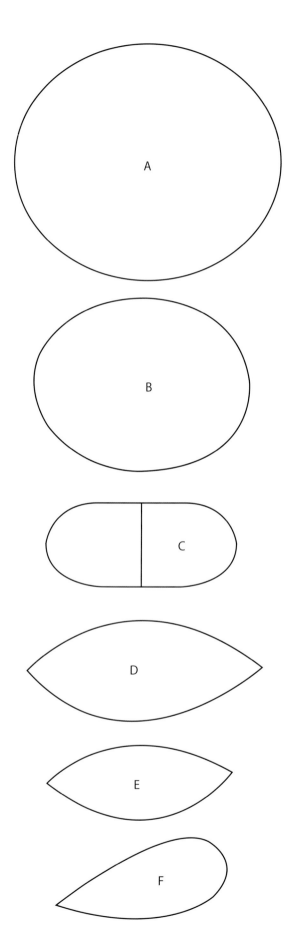

BLUEBELLS

I love to use Fossil Fern fabrics (by Bernartex) for this flower, using the lightest patch of the wrong side for the light and a dark patch of the right side for the dark.

You could choose to have either A or B dark; just be consistent with all the flowers.

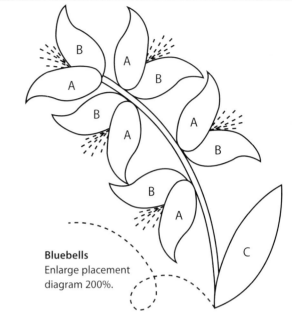

Bluebells
Enlarge placement diagram 200%.

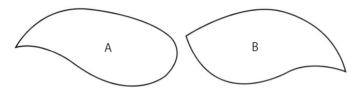

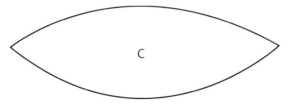

Refer to pages 7–11 for general appliqué information.

1. Trace only the design lines necessary for placing the appliqué pieces onto the background fabric.

2. Use freezer paper templates to make the petals A and B and leaf C.

3. Cut a ⅜″-wide bias strip for the stem. Appliqué the stem in place.

4. Appliqué the B petals in place; then add the A petals and leaf C. Use 3 strands of embroidery floss in a contrasting color to add embroidery details to the flowers. Add the tendril using 6 strands of floss. Seed pearls or beads are a nice finishing touch.

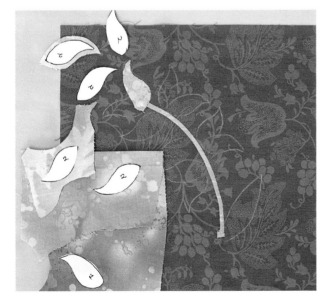

Prepare the pieces and appliqué stem.

Appliqué and add embroidery.

CHRYSANTHEMUM

This is one of my fiddliest flowers, no doubt about it! But in spite of its apparent complexity, it only uses two templates, so it is easy to construct. The center is perfect for fussy cutting.

Sometimes I use this technique with three layers of petals. I often embroider a small stab stitch around the entire flower as shown on the left.

Refer to pages 7–11 for general appliqué information.

1. Trace the design lines onto the background fabric. Accuracy is important on this flower.

2. Use Mylar templates to make the long A ovals (cut fabric in half after making) and the center oval B. Use a freezer paper template to make the leaf C. The calyx is also made using an oval template A. I used the same fabric for the calyx and the stem.

3. Cut a ⅜″-wide bias strip for the stem.

4. Appliqué the pieces in place, starting with the stem and calyx. Add the outer petals, following the marked lines, and then add the inner petals. Appliqué the center, making sure to cover all raw edges. Add the leaf and the embroidered tendril.

Appliqué the stem, calyx, and outer petals.

Stitch the center, leaf, and embroidery.

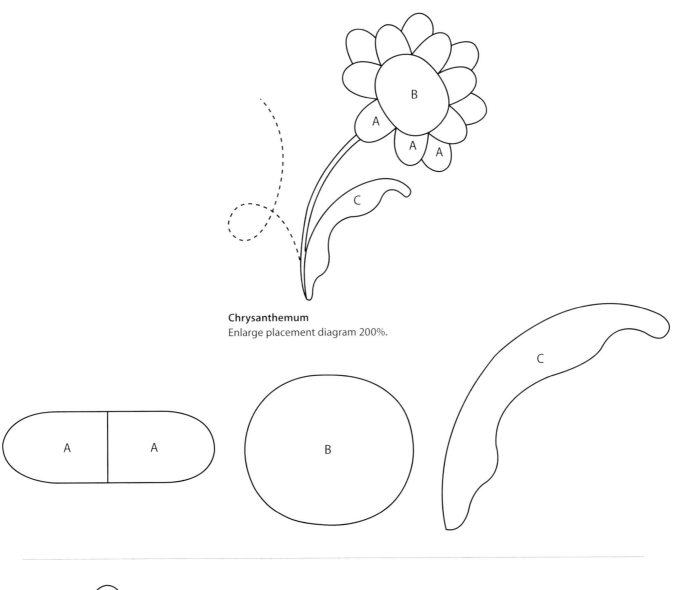

Chrysanthemum
Enlarge placement diagram 200%.

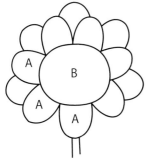

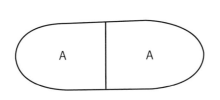

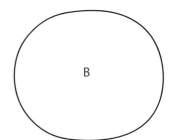

**Alternate flower for
Chrysanthemum Border** (page 105)
Enlarge placement diagram 200%.

DAHLIA

This exotic bloom looks great with graduating colored petals. You could further enhance it by fussy cutting the stamen heads.

Refer to pages 7–11 for general appliqué information.

1. Trace the design lines onto the background fabric.

2. Use Mylar templates to make C (stamen heads) and D (calyx). Cut D in half after pressing fabric to make 2 calyxes. Use freezer paper templates to make the petals A and B and leaves E and F.

3. Cut a ⅜″-wide bias strip for the stem.

4. Appliqué the stem and the calyx. Add the 2 inner petals, sewing to where the next petal will overlap. Trim the base of the petals as shown (lower left photo). Stitch the next pair of petals and again trim the bases.

5. Sew the final pair of petals, covering all raw ends of the inner petals. Use 3 strands of embroidery floss to make the stamens; then appliqué the stamen heads. Embroider the tendril using 6 strands of floss.

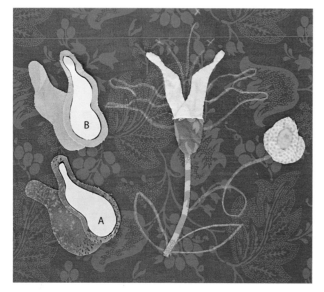

Prepare the appliqué pieces.

Appliqué the remaining petals, and add embroidery.

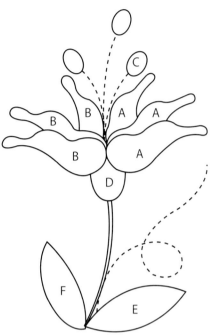

Dahlia
Enlarge placement diagram 200%.

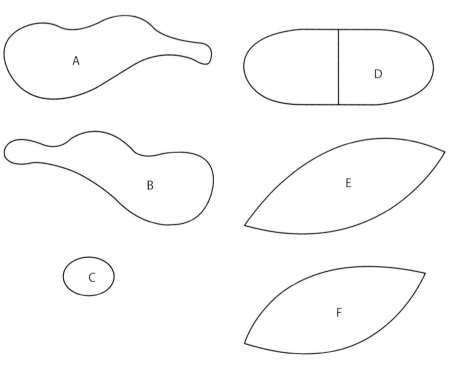

DAISY

I love to fussy cut daisy centers and will change the size of the flower centers to accommodate perfect finds! The fabrics shown here are ideal for flower centers.

Daisy center fabrics

Refer to pages 7–11 for general appliqué information.

1. Trace only the design lines necessary for placing the appliqué pieces onto the background fabric.

2. Use Mylar templates to make the petals B and flower center A. Use freezer paper templates to make the leaves C and D.

3. Cut a ⅜″-wide bias strip for the stem.

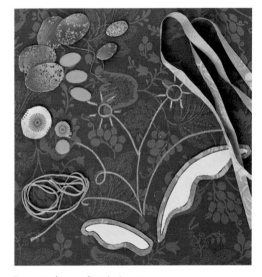

Prepare the appliqué pieces.

4. Appliqué the pieces in place, beginning with the stems; then add embroidery details.

Appliqué and add embroidery.

By altering the size and number of the petals, the size and placement of the centers, and the embroidery embellishment, you can create endless possibilities.

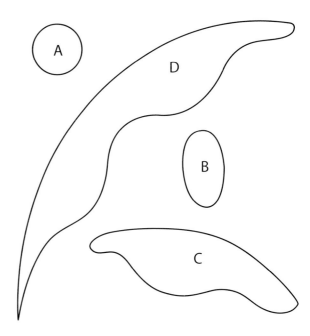

Simple Daisy
Enlarge placement diagram 200%.

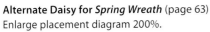

Alternate Daisy for *Spring Wreath* (page 63)
Enlarge placement diagram 200%.

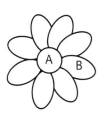

Alternate Daisy for *Harvest Wreath* (page 66)
Enlarge placement diagram 200%.

Alternate Daisy for
Butterfly and Berries (page 55) and
Simple Daisy and Hearts Border (page 103)
Enlarge placement diagram 200%.

FORGET-ME-NOT

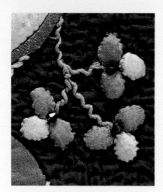

I love the Forget-Me-Not's delicacy. Although a lot of stitching around templates can seem onerous, it is well worth the effort. These flowers always add sparkle to a design, especially when made in white. Sometimes I add a crystal in the center of each flower for extra pizzazz.

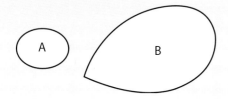

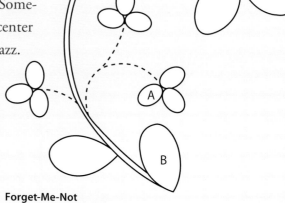

Forget-Me-Not
Enlarge placement diagram 200%.

Refer to pages 7–11 for general appliqué information.

1. Trace crosses onto the background fabric to indicate petal locations.

2. Use Mylar templates to make the petals A and freezer paper templates to make the leaves B.

3. Cut a ⅜″-wide bias strip for the stem.

4. Appliqué the petals in place. Then appliqué and embroider the stems. Stitch the leaves. Make a cross stitch in a contrasting color in the center between the petals of each cluster.

Appliqué and add embroidery.

Prepare the appliqué pieces.

FUCHSIA (SINGLE AND DOUBLE)

The single and the double fuchsia are fun to create—just let your fabrics guide you. This is a perfect opportunity for fussy cutting; you can adjust the size of your petals to accommodate the motif you want to fussy cut. The stamens can be created using embroidery, appliquéd circles, beads, or crystals.

Refer to pages 7–11 for general appliqué information.

Single Fuchsia

1. Trace only the design lines necessary for placing the appliqué pieces onto the background fabric.

2. Use freezer paper templates to make the petals A and leaves D. Use Mylar templates for the stamen heads B and calyx. I love to fussy cut 2 of the petals and the stamen heads.

3. Cut a ⅜″-wide bias strip for the stem.

Prepare the appliqué pieces.

4. Appliqué the pieces in place, starting with the stem and calyx, moving on to the 2 inner petals, and followed by the 2 outer petals on top. Be sure the petals meet in the center. Use 3 strands of embroidery floss to embroider the stamens; then appliqué the circular stamen heads on top.

Add the outer petals, stamens, leaves, and tendril.

> **TIP**
>
> *Baste the petals in place to be sure they meet nicely in the center.*

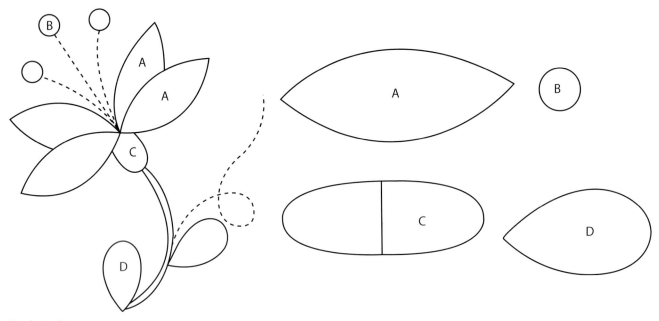

Single Fuchsia
Enlarge placement diagram 200%.

Double Fuchsia

1. Prepare the appliqués as you did for the Single Fuchsia (page 23).

2. Appliqué the stem and calyx first, then the top and bottom petals.

3. Add the 2 middle petals. Finish with a spray of embroidered stamens, sewn with 3 strands of embroidery floss.

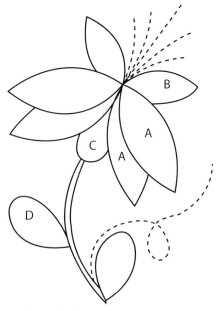

Double Fuchsia
Enlarge placement diagram 200%.

Sew the stem, calyx, and 4 petals.

Add the middle petals and leaves and embroider the stamens.

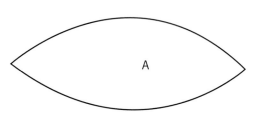

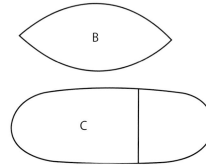

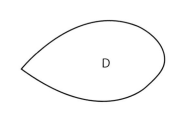

GRAPES / WISTERIA / HANGING BLOOMS

Grapes, in some form or other, appear in many of my quilts. Simple to make, they can be tweaked to make flowers both real and imagined. I usually use 10 grapes, but I have used up to 15 and have varied the oval shape from long and thin to plump.

The pattern that follows is fundamentally the bunch of grapes taken from *Butterfly and Berries* (page 55). However, with additional embroidery and circles, it becomes a sort of fantasy wisteria.

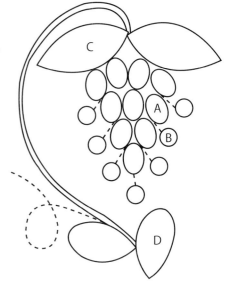

Grapes / Wisteria / Hanging Blooms
Enlarge placement diagram 200%.

Refer to pages 7–11 for general appliqué information.

1. Trace only the design lines necessary for placing the appliqué pieces onto the background fabric.

2. Use Mylar templates to make the circles B and ovals A and freezer paper templates to make the leaves C and D.

3. Cut a ⅜″-wide bias strip for the stem.

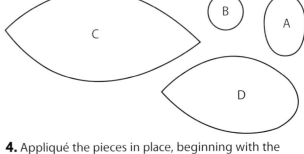

4. Appliqué the pieces in place, beginning with the stem. Then add embroidery details, using 6 strands of embroidery floss. Be sure to hide the stem end under the leaf where the top leaves meet and to always work bunches of grapes from the top grapes downward.

Prepare the appliqué pieces.

> ◾ **NOTE**
>
> *You could also add crystals, beads, or embroidery between the grapes or add more ovals in graduating colors.*

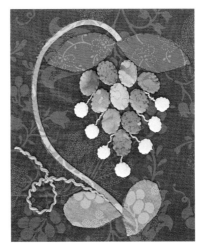

Appliqué and add embroidery.

Carefully look at your floral fabrics to see if you can fussy cut the flower center. The Iris works well in a solid or patterned fabric, too.

Refer to pages 7–11 for general appliqué information.

1. Trace the design lines onto the background fabric.

2. Use Mylar templates to make pieces F and G and freezer paper templates to make the petals A, B, C, D, and E and the leaves H and I.

3. Cut a ⅜″-wide bias strip for the stem.

4. Appliqué the stem and petals B, D, and E. Add petals A and C in place.

5. Sew G so it covers all raw ends of the other petals. Complete with embroidered stamens, using 3 strands of embroidery floss. Appliqué ovals F. Add leaves H and I.

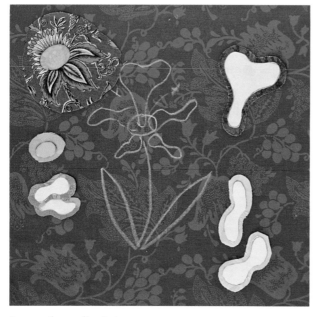

Prepare the appliqué pieces.

Appliqué and add embroidery.

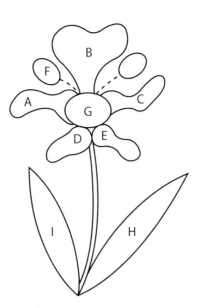

Iris
Enlarge placement diagram 200%.

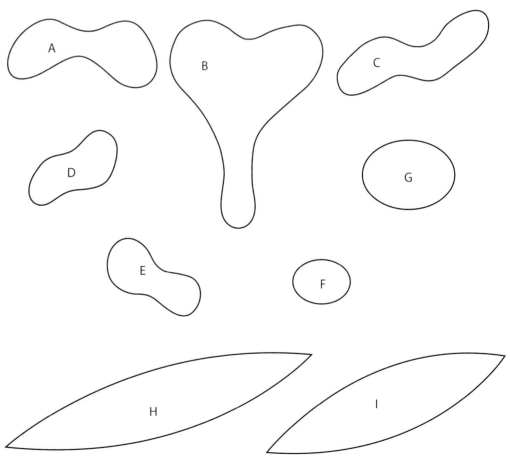

LILY

The Lily is a large and easy flower to construct. For the best effect, use petal fabrics in three values—dark, medium, and light.

Refer to pages 7–11 for general appliqué information.

1. Trace only the design lines necessary for placing the appliqué pieces onto the background fabric.

2. Use freezer paper templates to make the petals and leaf G. Cut petal F from dark fabric; A and E from medium fabric; and B, C, and D from light fabric.

3. Cut a ⅜″-wide bias strip for the stem.

> **TIP**
>
> *Baste the petals with a couple of centrally placed stitches to hold them in place. Trim and leave the edges raw where they will be covered by subsequent petals.*

4. Appliqué the pieces in place: first the stem; followed by F; then A, E, and C. Finally, add petals B and D. Embroider the petals with a running stitch, using 3 strands of embroidery floss. Add the leaf. Finish with a tendril and dramatic stamens, using a detached buttonhole stitch (page 9) at the end of 6 of the 7 stamens. Finish the central stamen with 3 glossy black beads or embroidery.

Appliqué the stem and petals F, A, E, and C.

Appliqué petals B and D and leaf G. Embroider the petals, stamens, and tendril.

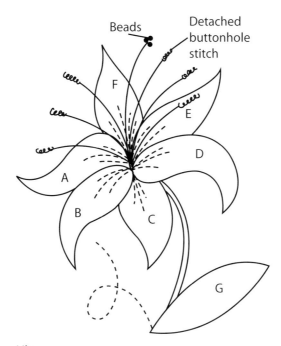

Beads

Detached buttonhole stitch

F

E

D

A

B

C

G

Lily
Enlarge placement diagram 200%.

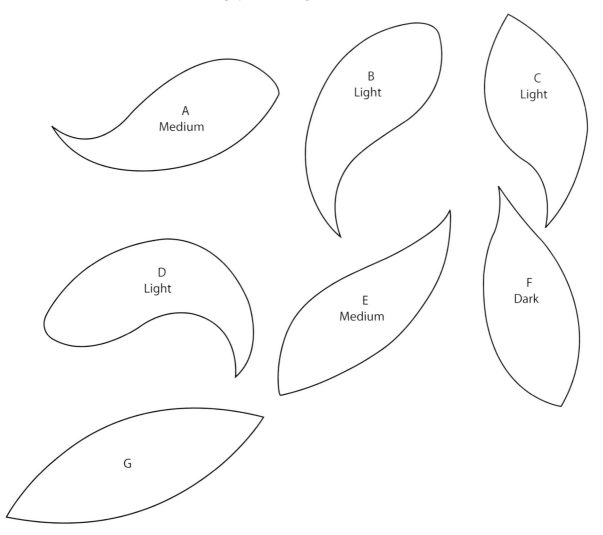

A
Medium

B
Light

C
Light

D
Light

E
Medium

F
Dark

G

MICHAELMAS DAISY / CONEFLOWER

The Michaelmas Daisy is one of the easiest flowers to sew, with its simple petal and center shapes. I love to use a spotty fabric for the flower head and to embroider small stitches around the top to give the dusty pollen look that I associate with daisies. Tweak the Michaelmas Daisy a bit by taking away a petal or two and you have the Coneflower.

Refer to pages 7–11 for general appliqué information.

1. Trace only the design lines necessary for placing the appliqué pieces onto the background fabric.

2. Use Mylar templates to make the flower center B and freezer paper templates to make the petals A and leaves C and D. Although the petals are all slightly different, you only need to cut one template A shape. You will adapt this shape to your marked petals.

3. Cut a ⅜″-wide bias strip for the stem.

4. Appliqué the pieces in place, starting with the stem and then the petals, working from the outside in. Sew the flower center, covering all raw edges. Add the leaves. Make tiny stitches around the daisy head, using 3 strands of embroidery thread. Stitch the tendril.

> ■ **NOTE**
>
> *The petal size, quantity, as well as the center, and embroidery can be modified to change the look of this flower. A few variations are provided on page 31.*

Appliqué the stem and petals.

Appliqué flower center and leaves, and add embroidery.

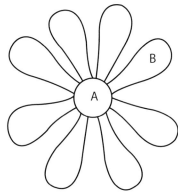

Michaelmas Daisy
Enlarge placement diagram 200%.

Alternate Michaelmas Daisy for
Mexican Heart (page 77)
Enlarge placement diagram 200%.

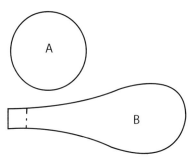

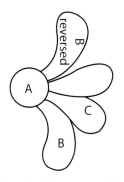

Alternate Michaelmas Daisy for
Mexican Heart (page 77)
Enlarge placement diagram 200%.

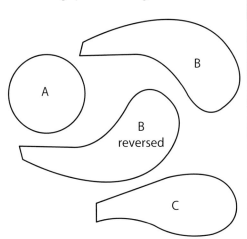

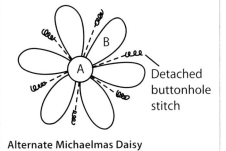

Detached
buttonhole
stitch

Alternate Michaelmas Daisy
(with petal shape options) for
Fuchsia Border and Corner Design
(page 104)
Enlarge placement diagram 200%.

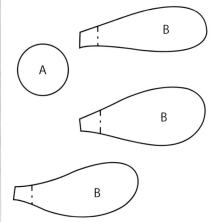

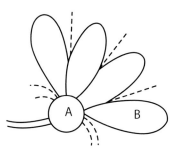

Alternate Coneflower for
Harvest Wreath (page 66)
Enlarge placement diagram 200%.

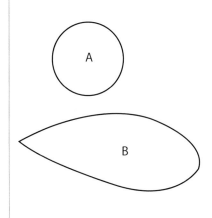

MIMOSA / FLORAL SPRAY / BERRIES

It doesn't get much easier in terms of skill, and yet this flower is always one of the most eye-catching and most appreciated flowers in all my quilts, whether masquerading as a spray of wheat, oats, grasses, mimosa, or wisteria.

The Floral Spray and Berries templates (page 33) are ovals. Mimosa should, strictly speaking, be made from graduated circles—something I must try one day! By adding embroidery and seed pearls, this flower spray can become very exotic and decorative. I usually use three to five shades of color, but it would work with fewer—even just one color works.

Refer to pages 7–11 for general appliqué information.

1. Trace only the design lines necessary for placing the appliqué pieces onto the background fabric.

2. Use Mylar templates to make the ovals. Use freezer paper templates to make the leaves.

3. Cut ⅜"-wide bias strips for the stems.

4. Appliqué the pieces in place—first the stems and berries, then the leaves. Add embroidery details. In this example, I added 3 Lazy Daisy stitches at the end of each oval.

Prepare the appliqué pieces.

Appliqué and add embroidery.

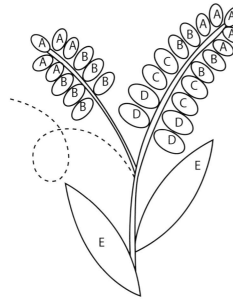
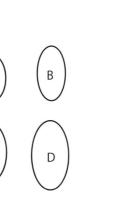
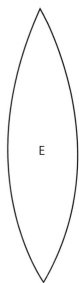

Mimosa / Floral Spray / Berries
Enlarge placement diagram 200%.

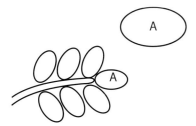

Alternate Berries for
Spring Wreath (page 63)
Enlarge placement diagram 200%.

Alternate Berries for
Baltimore Beauty and Bluebells
pillow (page 61)
Enlarge placement diagram 200%.

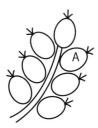

Alternate Berries for
Butterfly and Berries **pillow** (page 55)
Enlarge placement diagram 200%.

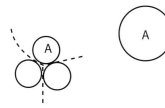

Alternate Berries for
Butterfly and Berries (page 55) and
Vine Fruits (page 81)
Enlarge placement diagram 200%.

Alternate Berries for
Harvest Wreath (page 66)
Enlarge placement diagram 200%.

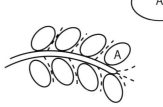

Alternate Berries for
Star Flower Heart (page 74)
Enlarge placement diagram 200%.

PANSY

In nature, the huge variety of colors of pansies makes it a good flower for adding a bit of punch to a quilt design. I like to keep this flower delicate and usually in groups of three. I often use six strands of embroidery floss to make the pansy stems.

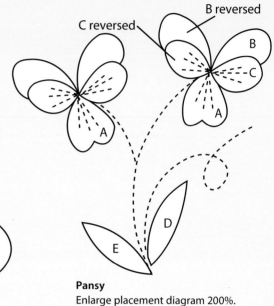

Pansy
Enlarge placement diagram 200%.

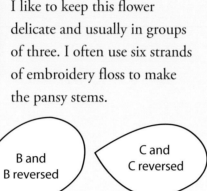

Refer to pages 7–11 for general appliqué information.

1. Trace the design lines onto the background fabric.

2. Use freezer paper templates to make the petals A, B, and C and the leaves D and E. Use 3 different colors of fabric for the petals.

3. Embroider the stems, and then appliqué petal A, covering the stem ends.

4. Appliqué both B petals, making sure they meet at the point of the heart.

5. Stitch both C petals so they meet at the point of petal A, slightly below the meeting point of the B petals. Then add the leaves.

6. Embroider the petal details with 2 strands of embroidery floss in a contrasting color. Add an embroidered tendril with 6 strands of floss.

Embroider stems and add A and B petals.

Appliqué the C petals and leaves and add embroidery.

PEONY

This is one of the more time-consuming flowers to appliqué. I graduate the colors in the petals to prevent the look of a large block of color. I've added a fancy calyx to the peony shown on the left, but it's just as beautiful without it (below). When drawing this template, I had in mind the peonies that grew in our garden in England—great snowballs of feathery petals.

Refer to pages 7–11 for general appliqué information.

1. Trace all design lines onto the background fabric.

2. Use freezer paper templates to make the petals and leaf L.

NOTE

If you use both sides of a variegated fabric and strategically place the templates, you can get a dark-to-light effect from the center petal (K) outward.

Petals on variegated fabric

Appliqué petals, working from the outside to the center.

3. Cut a ⅜″-wide bias strip for the stem.

TIP

Baste the petals with a couple of centrally placed stitches to hold them in place. Trim and leave the edges raw where they will be covered by subsequent petals.

---

4. Appliqué the pieces in place, starting with the stem and then adding the petals and leaf. Add an embroidered tendril.

Finish appliqué and embroider the tendril.

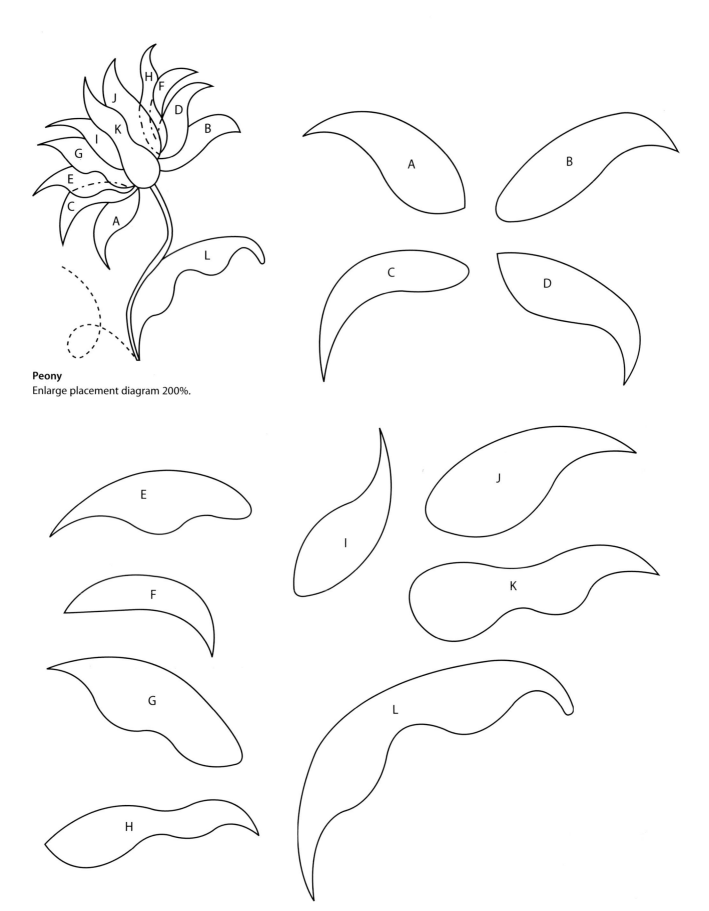

Peony
Enlarge placement diagram 200%.

POMEGRANATE

I am so fond of the simplicity of this pomegranate, and I love the fact that people immediately identify it. It is very easy to appliqué. You can have a lot of fun with the center. Red dots or spots are irresistible. Use some fine beading to represent the seeds.

Refer to pages 7–11 for general appliqué information.

1. Trace only the design lines necessary for placing the appliqué pieces onto the background fabric. You need not mark B and C.

2. Use Mylar templates to make A, B, C, and the calyx. Use freezer paper templates to make the crown petals D, E, and F, and the leaf G. Cut the fabric calyx piece in half after pressing to make 2.

3. Cut a ⅜˝-wide bias strip for the stem.

Prepare the appliqué pieces.

4. Appliqué the stem, calyx, and crown petals in order: D, F, and E.

5. Baste A in place and appliqué so it covers the raw edges of the crown petals and calyx.

Baste A in place.

6. Add B. Sew C in place, leaving a small part of the inside layer of B showing at both ends. Add the leaf and the embroidered tendril.

Appliqué B, C, and the leaf G. Add embroidery.

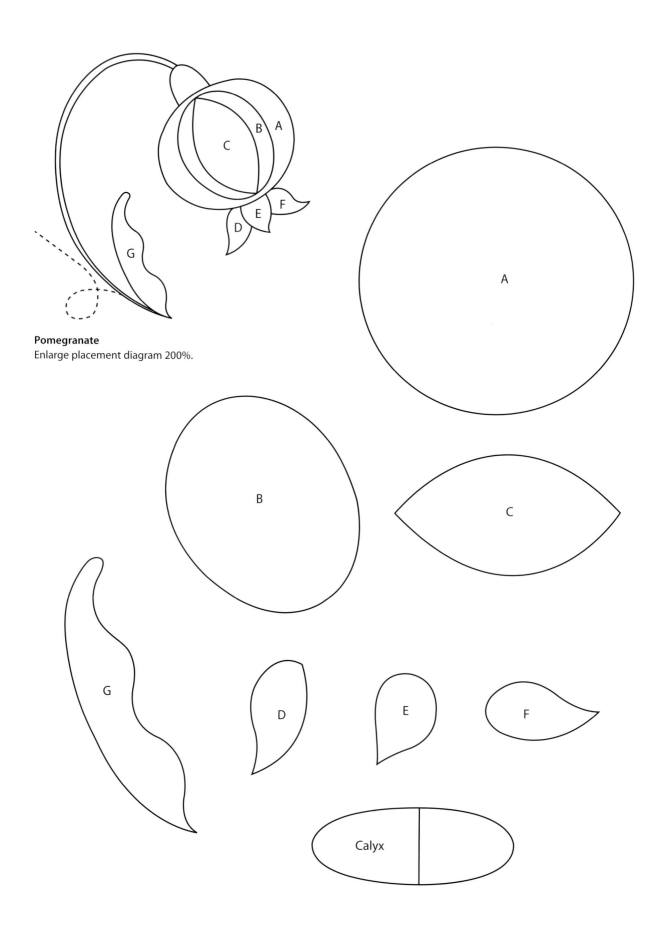

Pomegranate
Enlarge placement diagram 200%.

A

B

C

G

D

E

F

Calyx

STAR FLOWER

With its potential for high color contrast between the circle of rounded petals and the circle of pointed petals, this flower can have a big "wow factor." For a quieter look, use two values of one color for the two differently shaped petals. The center circle is perfect for fussy cutting. Combined with its simple embroidery, this flower can add a great deal of interest and detail to a project.

Refer to pages 7–11 for general appliqué information.

1. Trace the design onto the background fabric.

2. Use Mylar templates to make the flower center and the C petals. Cut fabric for C petals in half after pressing. Each C makes 2 petals. Use freezer paper templates to make the B petals and leaves. I love to fussy cut both the center and the rounded petals.

3. Cut a ⅜"-wide bias strip for the stem.

4. Follow the marked lines to sew the stem and a complete ring of C petals. Then appliqué the B petals on top.

5. Cover all the raw ends with the center. Add the leaves.

6. Use 3 strands of embroidery floss to embroider the center line on the petals with a whipstitch (pages 8 and 9). Use 6 strands to embroider the tendril.

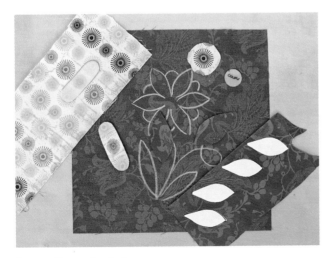

Prepare the appliqué pieces.

Complete the appliqué and add embroidery.

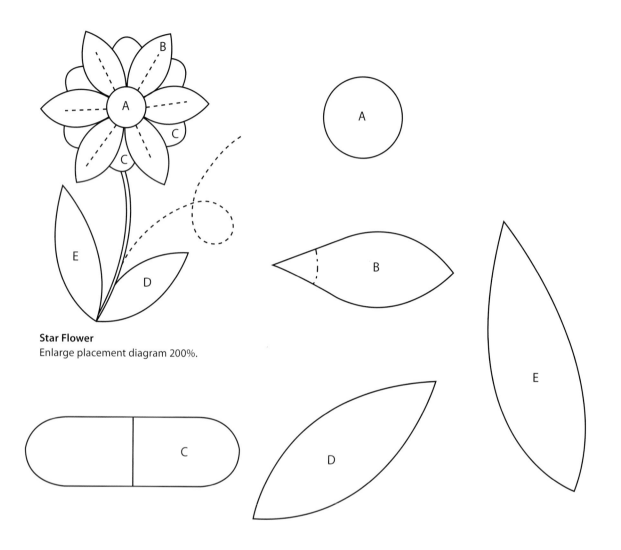

Star Flower
Enlarge placement diagram 200%.

STARGAZER LILY

Whereas most of my flowers are representational or straight out of my head, this pattern was a deliberate attempt to create a realistic lily for a silk lily wreath I designed. In the example, I added some dimension by using the right side of the fabric for petals A, C, and E and the wrong (lighter) side for petals B, D, and F.

Refer to pages 7–11 for general appliqué information.

1. Trace the design lines onto the background fabric as accurately as possible for placing the appliqué pieces. You will be following these lines closely.

2. Use freezer paper templates to make the petals and leaves. Draw each petal carefully along the inner edge to prevent the marked lines from showing.

3. Cut a ⅜″-wide bias strip for the stem.

4. Stitch the stem; then carefully follow the pencil lines to appliqué petals A, C, and E. Leave unstitched any areas where petals will be covered by B, D, and F. Add petals B, D, and F.

5. Embroider 7 stamens with 3 strands of embroidery floss. Use a detached buttonhole stitch (page 9) to make heavy orange anthers on 6 stamen stems. Sew 3 black beads for the central stamen anther.

Appliqué the stem and petals A, C, and E.

Complete the appliqué and add embroidery.

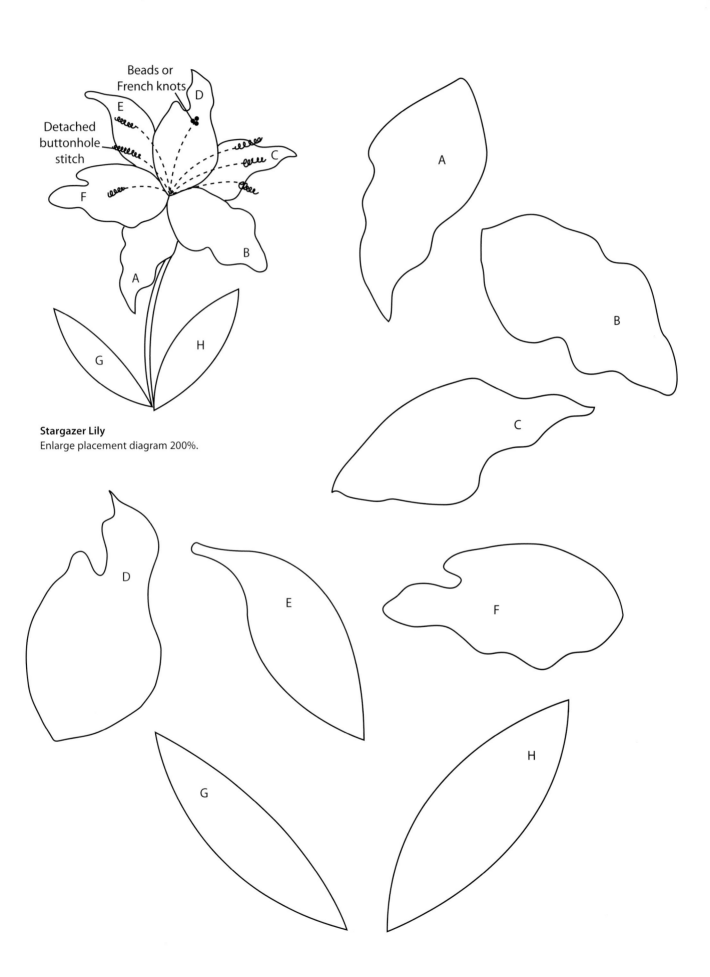

Beads or
French knots

Detached
buttonhole
stitch

Stargazer Lily
Enlarge placement diagram 200%.

SUNFLOWER / ASTER / ZINNIA

This flower may be time-consuming to make, but it is especially effective if you fussy cut the large central circle. The trick is good fabric selection for the petals. Ideally you need three or four different tones to add depth for the petals. Hand dyes or Fossil Fern fabrics are perfect, especially if you use the reverse side for lighter tones.

Refer to pages 7–11 for general appliqué information.

1. Trace only the design lines necessary for placing the appliqué pieces onto the background fabric.

2. Use a Mylar template to make the flower center A. Use freezer paper templates to make the petals and leaf B. Stack or fold your petal fabrics, iron freezer paper petal templates on top on the bias, and cut out as many petals as desired, leaving a ¼˝ seam allowance. Clip the inner curves to the paper. By folding the fabric, you will create a possibility of 4 different shapes (if you use the wrong side of the fabric). This will give you a variety of shapes and colors to help you achieve the most effective flower.

3. Cut a ⅜˝-wide bias strip for the stem.

4. Appliqué the pieces in place: first the stem, petals, and leaf, and then the flower center. Add the embroidered tendril.

To make the flower head, you don't need to follow the illustration exactly as drawn. Instead, you can fill around the center circle with as many petals as desired, using a variety of shapes and colors until the circle is complete.

Appliqué the stem, petals, and leaf; then embroider the tendril. Appliqué the center circle.

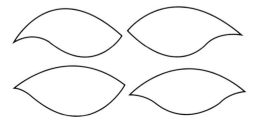

Use petals in any combination.

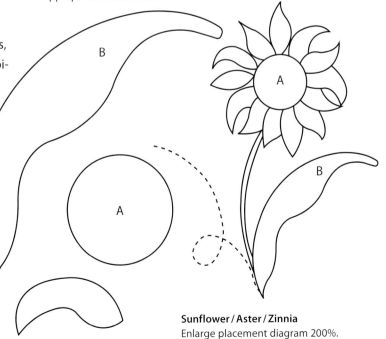

Sunflower / Aster / Zinnia
Enlarge placement diagram 200%.

SWEET WILLIAM

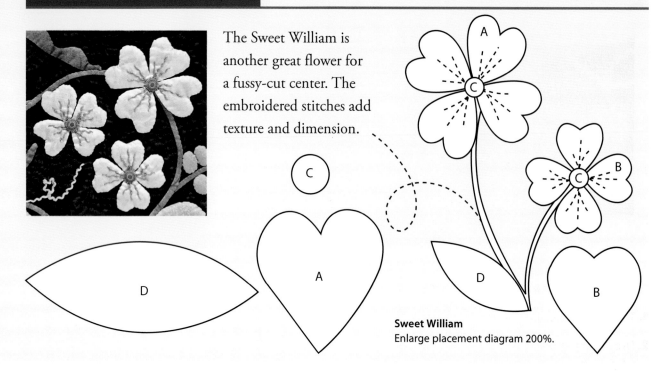

The Sweet William is another great flower for a fussy-cut center. The embroidered stitches add texture and dimension.

C

A

D

Sweet William
Enlarge placement diagram 200%.

Refer to pages 7–11 for general appliqué information.

1. Trace the design lines onto the background fabric.

2. Use Mylar templates to make the flower center C. Use freezer paper templates to make the petals A and B and leaf D.

3. Cut ⅜″-wide bias strips for the stems. Appliqué the stems.

4. Baste each petal with a couple of loose stitches in the petal center for easier stitching, and then appliqué all 4 petals.

5. Appliqué the center; then add embroidery details to the petals. Add the leaf and embroider the tendril.

Appliqué and add embroidery.

Prepare the pieces and appliqué the stems.

WHIRLED FLOWER

I like to make this flower with a fussy-cut center and two or three fabrics for the petals.

Refer to pages 7–11 for general appliqué information.

1. Trace the design lines onto the background fabric.

2. Use Mylar templates to make the flower center F. Use freezer paper templates to make the petals A, B, C, D, and E and leaf G.

3. Cut a ⅜″-wide bias strip for the stem.

4. Appliqué petal A in place along the underside of the petal that will be covered by petal B. Stop at the point marked X (see template pattern, page 46).

Appliqué the stem and petals.

5. Add petal B, and then the stem. Continue to sew on all the petals, including petal E.

6. Finish stitching petal A by slipstitching on top of petal E. Cover all raw ends with the flower center. Add the leaf. Embroider the tendril.

Partially appliqué petal A.

Complete appliqué and add embroidery.

Whirled Flower
Enlarge placement diagram 200%.

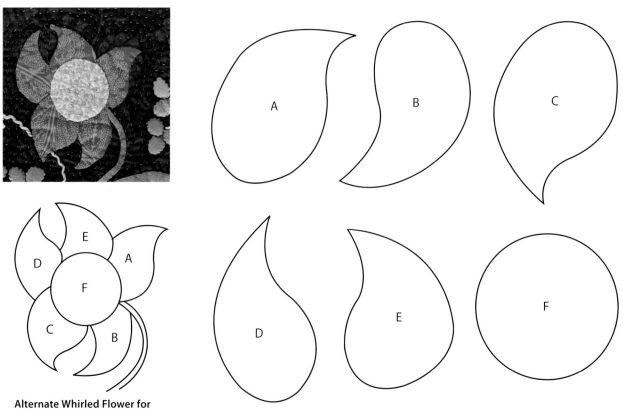

Alternate Whirled Flower for
Forget-Me-Nots and Pansies
pillow (page 59)
Enlarge placement diagram 200%.

EASY TEMPLATE FLOWERS

With some imaginative fussy cutting and strategic embroidery, you can make highly decorative flowers with the simplest of shapes.

Refer to pages 7–11 for general appliqué information.

1. Use Mylar templates to make the petals.

2. Cut a ⅜″-wide bias strip for the stem, or use embroidery.

3. Appliqué the pieces in place and add embroidery details.

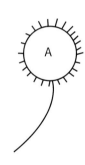

Enlarge placement diagrams 200%.

Enlarge placement diagram 200%.

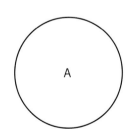

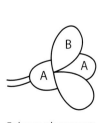

Enlarge placement diagram 200%.

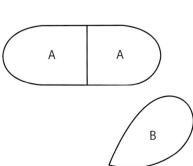

Detached buttonhole stitch

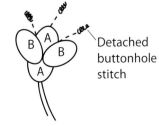
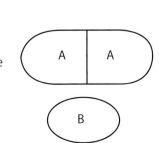

Enlarge placement diagram 200%.

BUTTERFLY

This is my simplest butterfly. If I'm trying to use a fabric more successfully, I may change the size of the butterfly; otherwise, the basic shape remains the same. You can make a butterfly from solids and fussy-cut floral fabrics, or you can cut your template pattern pieces from the fantastic printed butterfly fabrics that are available.

Butterfly fabrics

Refer to pages 7–11 for general appliqué information.

1. Trace the basic butterfly shape onto the background fabric.

2. Use Mylar to make head B and abdomen C and freezer paper templates to make 4 wings.

3. Appliqué the bottom 2 wings and then the upper wings. Trim the overlap in the center that will be covered by abdomen C.

4. Add B and C. Embroider the antennae and sew a bead on each end.

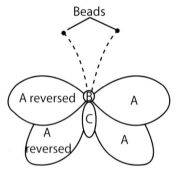

Large Butterfly
Enlarge placement diagram 200%.

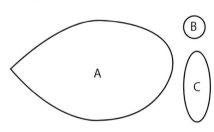

Prepare the appliqué pieces.

Appliqué and embellish.

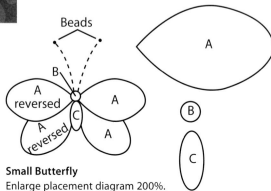

Small Butterfly
Enlarge placement diagram 200%.

48   BEAUTIFUL BOTANICALS

NOSEGAY

The Nosegay is less of a bloom and more of a posy!
I designed this flower for those of you who might
want to try a very small project for a pillow with
one of the borders.

Refer to pages 7–11 for general appliqué information.

1. Trace the design onto the background fabric.

2. Use Mylar templates to make A, B, and D and freezer
paper templates to make the petals and leaves.

3. Cut a ⅜″-wide bias strip for the stem.

4. Appliqué the stems and then the leaves. Then
appliqué the flowers, berries, and buds.

Appliqué the stems.

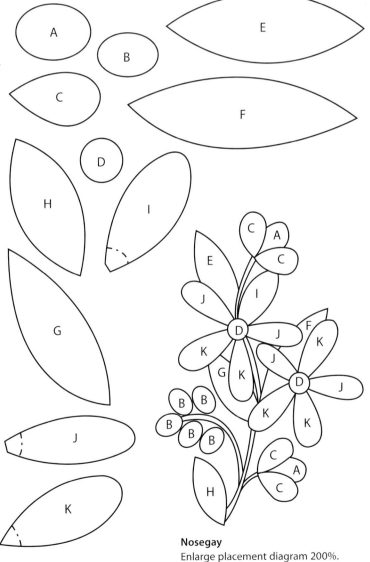

Nosegay
Enlarge placement diagram 200%.

ADDITIONAL LEAF TEMPLATES

Here is a selection of the leaf templates used in the projects. You can either match the leaf size as designated by the pattern or use larger or smaller leaves.

Refer to pages 7–11 for general appliqué information.

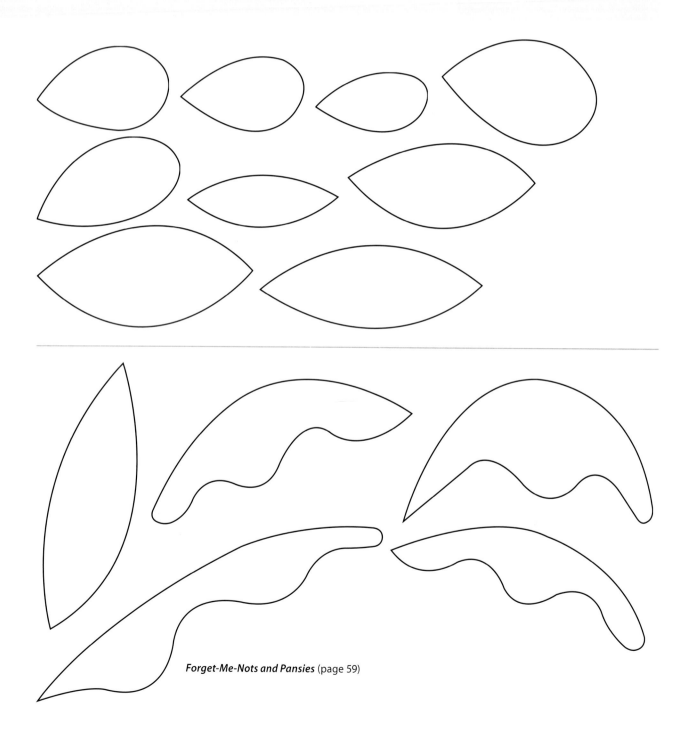

Forget-Me-Nots and Pansies (page 59)

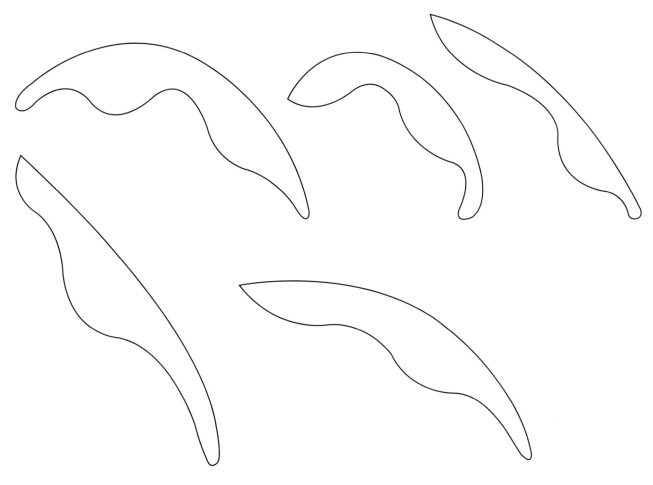

Autumn Tiger Lily with Asters (page 57)

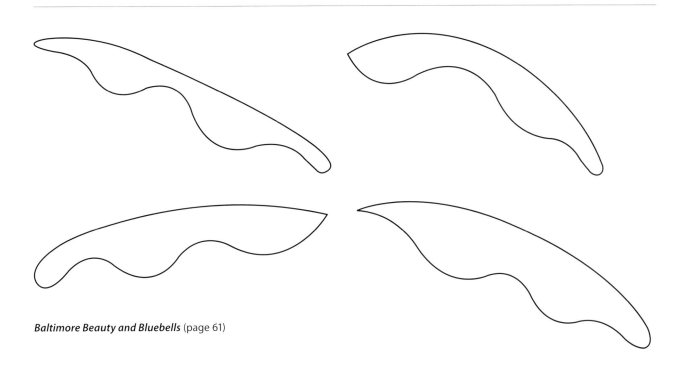

Baltimore Beauty and Bluebells (page 61)

Butterfly and Berries (page 55)

Forget-Me-Nots and Pansies (page 59)

Autumn Tiger Lily with Asters (page 57)

Baltimore Beauty and Bluebells (page 61)

PART 2: THE PROJECTS

17¹/₂˝ × 17¹/₂˝ PILLOWS

The four designs that follow have 13″ central blocks surrounded by a simple 1″ finished sawtooth inner border and a plain 1″ finished outer border. Fabric requirements and instructions are for making each of the pillows with an envelope-style opening on the back and are identical for all four pillows. I use a 16″ pillow insert, but you could use an 18″ insert for a firmer pillow. These designs can also be finished as wallhanging quilts.

17½″ × 17½″ pillow or quilt top

Materials and Cutting

1 yard of fabric for background, outer border, and pillow backing

Cut:

1 square 15″ × 15″ for pillow front; trim to 13½″ × 13½″ after appliquéing

12 pieces 2″ × 6″; subcut into 56 background triangles for foundation-pieced sawtooth border (pages 100–102)

4 squares 1½″ × 1½″ for sawtooth border corners

2 pieces 12″ × 17½″ for pillow backing

2 strips 1½″ × 15½″ for outer border sides

2 strips 1½″ × 17½″ for outer border top/bottom

14″ × 14″ square of fabric for stems

Cut:

⅜″-wide bias strips for stems, as shown.

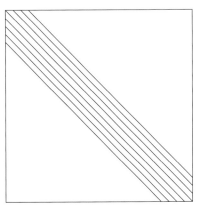

Cut ⅜″-wide bias strips.

1 yard total of assorted prints and solid fabric for flowers and saw-tooth triangles

Cut:

11 pieces 2″ × 6″; subcut into 52 triangles for foundation-pieced border (pages 100–102)

22″ × 22″ square of muslin for backing (This will be inside the pillow, so it will not show.)

22″ × 22″ square of batting

⅛ yard of fabric for binding

Cut:

2 strips 1″ wide for 80″ continuous single-fold binding

Mylar heatproof template plastic

Freezer paper

Fabric-marking pencil and eraser

Foundation paper

Embroidery floss in minimum of 3 colors or as desired

Beads and seed pearls (*optional*)

16″ pillow form (Use an 18″ pillow form if you prefer a firmer pillow.)

> ### ■ NOTE
>
> *All templates for the projects in Part 2 can be found in Part 1: The Flowers (pages 12–51). If desired, to make it easier to trace placement lines, enlarge the patterns by the percent specified to make the pattern full size.*

Construction

Refer to pages 7–11 for general appliqué information.

CENTER

1. Trace the center appliqué design onto the background fabric.

2. Use Mylar and freezer paper templates to make the appliqués.

3. Appliqué or embroider all the stems; then add the appliqué and embroidery as directed for the individual flowers in Part 1: The Flowers (pages 12–51).

4. Erase all pencil lines and press carefully with a hot iron. Trim to 13½˝ × 13½˝.

BORDERS

1. Prepare 4 paper foundation strips for a finished size of 1˝ × 13˝ (pages 100–102). Starting and finishing with the background-colored triangles, make the foundation-pieced strips and trim to 1½˝ × 13½˝.

2. With the colored triangles pointing away from the center, sew 2 strips to the sides of the central square, using a ¼˝ seam allowance. Press the seam allowance toward the center.

3. Sew a 1½˝ × 1½˝ background-colored square to each end of the 2 remaining strips. Press the seam allowance toward the squares.

4. Sew the remaining strips to the top and bottom. Press the seam allowance toward the triangles.

5. Sew 1½˝ × 15½˝ strips to the sides, pressing the seam allowance toward the inner border. Sew a 1½˝ × 17½˝ strip to the top and bottom. Press toward the inner border.

6. Press well. Then remove the foundation paper. Appliqué any motifs on the borders, if appropriate.

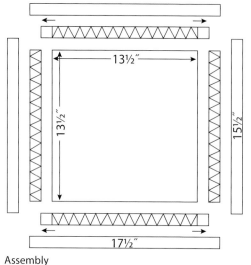

Assembly

FINISHING

1. Layer with batting and muslin; then baste the layers together. Quilt as desired. I chose to echo quilt throughout the central design and to outline quilt the triangles.

2. For the pillow back, fold over ¼˝ along the long edge and then fold over again ½˝. Topstitch close to the first fold. Repeat for the other backing piece. With right sides down, overlap the folded edges and adjust the overlap so that the pieces form a 17½˝ × 17½˝ square.

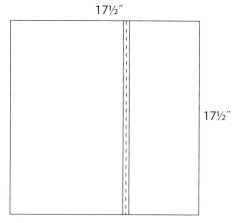

Pillow back

3. Place the pillow top right side up on the backing, with wrong sides together. Pin and baste ⅛˝ from the edge all the way around.

4. Stitch the binding strips together into one long strip. Fold under ¼˝ at one end of the binding strip. Starting at the center of one side, sew the binding all the way around the pillow, using a ¼˝ seam allowance. Overlap the ends by ½˝ and trim. Fold over ¼˝ along the raw edge of the binding and blindstitch to the back.

BUTTERFLY AND BERRIES
PILLOW

I love the soft-colored leaves on a soft red background. Choose the colors for the three main motifs first—the Pomegranate, bunch of Grapes, and a large Single Fuchsia—balancing both color and value. The daisies in white or light tones will always add sparkle, and the groups of three berries and daisy centers are ideal for fussy cutting. The stem color should contrast strongly with the background. If you decide to use green leaves, use three values—dark, medium, and light. Choose embroidery floss in the same color as the stem for the Daisy and Berry group stems and in contrasting colors for the tendrils and other embellishments.

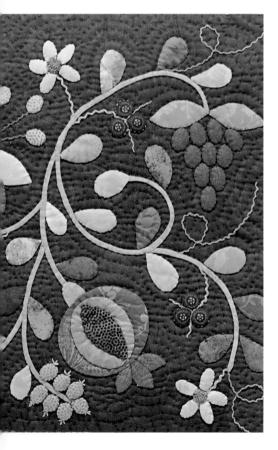

Enlarge the pattern by 400% to trace the full-size design on the background fabric.

AUTUMN TIGER LILY WITH ASTERS
PILLOW/QUILT

Deep purple sets off fall colors so beautifully, and this Fossil Fern fabric was an ideal choice. Golden green chartreuse stems contrast well, as do the three leaf values in green and gold. For a less scrappy effect, neither the stem nor the leaf colors are used in the foundation border. For the Lily and Floral Sprays, I used three values of each color—dark, medium, and light. I added tiny seed pearls to the end of the embroidery in the Floral Sprays. I cut the large Butterfly from butterfly fabric and placed a tiny crystal at the end of each antenna. I used all six strands of contrasting embroidery floss for the tendrils. For all other embroidery, I used three strands in coordinating colors.

Enlarge the pattern by 400% to trace the full-size design on the background fabric.

FORGET-ME-NOTS AND PANSIES
PILLOW

With this inky green-black background, all colors will sparkle and jump out at the viewer. I chose a high-contrast green for the stems and three values for the leaves—dark, medium, and light. For a less scrappy look, I didn't use any of the greens in the foundation border. The Fossil Fern fabric adds interest to the groups of three petals that make up the Forget-Me-Nots; I tried to make sure that the petals varied from each other in value. For the high-contrast embroidered tendrils in lime green, I used all six strands of floss. The Chrysanthemum center calls out for fussy cutting! I embroidered a checkerboard pattern in the center of the Whirled Flower, but a fussy-cut center would work equally well. I used a soft white for the long sprays of Berries to add high contrast and interest.

Enlarge the pattern by 400% to trace the full-size design on the background fabric.

BALTIMORE BEAUTY
AND BLUEBELLS
PILLOW

The colors of this pillow match the preceding pattern. I kept the same green-black background and used some similar colors for the flowers. The Bluebells use light and dark values and were cut from one piece of Fossil Fern fabric, using the wrong side of the fabric for a lighter value. The stem uses a high-contrast bright green, while the leaves are from three values—dark, medium, and light—as in *Forget-Me-Nots and Pansies* (page 59). No greens are used in the foundation border. The Baltimore Beauty Flower and Sweet William both have fussy-cut centers, and the embroidery for the Sweet William flowers coordinates with the centers.

Enlarge the pattern by 400% to trace the full-size design on the background fabric.

SPRING WREATH
PILLOW

16″ × 16″ pillow/quilt top

The Easter-colored lilac silk background and spring pastel flowers of this pillow will brighten any room. The pattern can easily fit a 16″ × 16″ pillow form or be extended with an 18″ × 18″ background to fit a similarly-sized pillow form.

Single Fuchsia (pages 23–24)

Alternate Mimosa / Floral Spray / Berries (pages 32–33)

Alternate Daisy (pages 20–21)

Materials and Cutting

1 yard of fabric for background, backing, and binding

Cut:

1 square 17″ × 17″ for background; trim to 16″ × 16″ after appliquéing

2 pieces 9″ × 16″ for pillow back

(If working with dupioni silk, baste the edges before appliquéing to prevent excessive fraying.)

2 strips 1″ wide for 74″ continuous single-fold binding

14″ × 14″ square of fabric for stems

Cut:

⅜″-wide bias strips, as needed *(Refer to page 53 for cutting bias strips.)*

Scraps of fabric with at least 2 values of green for appliqué

20″ × 20″ square of batting

20″ × 20″ square of fabric for backing

Mylar heatproof template plastic

Freezer paper

Fabric-marking pencil and eraser

3 colors of embroidery floss

16″ × 16″ pillow form

16″ zipper

Construction

Refer to pages 7–11 for general appliqué information.

CENTER

1. Trace the design onto the background fabric.

2. Use Mylar and freezer paper templates to make the appliqués.

3. Appliqué the stems first, starting with the stems that radiate to the outside of the central circle. Then appliqué the 4 stems that make up the circle and radiate inward. Cover the raw edges of previously sewn stems as you go.

4. Add the appliqué and embroidery, as directed for the individual flowers in Part 1: The Flowers (pages 12–51).

5. Embellish with embroidery, using 6 strands of floss for tendrils and 3 strands for all other embroidery.

6. Erase all pencil lines and press well.

FINISHING

1. Layer with batting and backing; quilt as desired.

2. Insert the zipper between the 2 back pieces of the pillow and trim to 16″ × 16″.

3. Pin the back to the front, wrong sides together, and baste ⅛″ from edge.

4. Stitch the binding strips together into one long strip. Fold under ¼″ at one end of the binding strip. Starting in the center of one side, sew the binding around the pillow, using a ¼″ seam allowance. Overlap the ends by ½″ and trim. Fold over ¼″ along the raw edge and blindstitch to the back.

Enlarge the pattern by 400% to trace the full-size design on the background fabric.

HARVEST WREATH
PILLOW

16″ × 16″ pillow top

This pillow combines dupioni silks with more traditional quilting fabrics. I love how the golden yellow dupioni silk glows next to the blue cotton.

This design uses a lot of Mylar templates, so if you are a fan of making ovals and circles, this is the pattern for you! Fussy-cut flower centers add an element of interest to this simple design.

Fussy-cut flower centers

Alternate Coneflower (pages 30–31)

Easy Template Flowers (page 47)

Alternate Mimosa / Floral Spray / Berries (pages 32–33)

Alternate Daisy (pages 20–21)

Materials and Cutting

¾ yard of fabric for background, pillow back, and binding

Cut:

1 square 17″ × 17″ for background; trim to 16″ × 16″ after appliquéing

2 pieces 9″ × 16″ for pillow back

(If working with dupioni silk, baste the edges before appliquéing to prevent excessive fraying.)

2 strips 1″ wide for 74″ continuous single-fold binding

14″ × 14″ square of fabric for stems

Cut:

⅜″-wide bias strips, as needed *(Refer to page 53 for cutting bias strips.)*

Scraps of fabric with at least 2 values of green for appliqué

20″ × 20″ square of batting

20″ × 20″ square of fabric for backing

Mylar heatproof template plastic

Freezer paper

Fabric-marking pencil and eraser

Embroidery floss

16″ × 16″ pillow form

16″ zipper

Construction

Refer to pages 7–11 for general appliqué information.

CENTER

1. Trace the design onto the background fabric.

2. Use Mylar and freezer paper templates to make the appliqués.

3. Appliqué the 4 stems that make up the circle and radiate inward. Cover the raw edges of previously sewn stems as you go.

4. Add the appliqué and embroidery as directed for the individual flowers in Part 1: The Flowers (pages 12–51).

5. Embellish with embroidery, using 6 strands of floss for the tendrils and 3 strands for all other embroidery.

6. Erase all pencil lines and press well.

FINISHING

1. Layer with batting and backing; quilt as desired.

2. Insert the zipper between the 2 back pieces of the pillow and trim to 16″ × 16″.

3. Pin the back to the front, wrong sides together, and baste ⅛″ from edge.

4. Stitch the binding strips together into one long strip. Fold under ¼″ at one end of the binding strip. Starting in the center of one side, sew the binding all around the pillow, using a ¼″ seam allowance. Overlap the ends of the binding by ½″ and trim. Fold over ¼″ along the raw edge and blind-stitch to the back.

Enlarge the pattern by 400% to trace the full-size design on the background fabric.

JACOBEAN TREE OF LIFE
WALLHANGING

18½″ × 18½″ quilt top

14″ × 14″ center block

This quilt and its pillow variation (page 73) beautifully illustrate just how different the same pattern can appear! Notice that the flowers on the trees are different. This was my first pattern design, and I used it to teach basic appliqué to my quilting group in Venezuela. The appliqué itself is as easy as can be, and this pattern works in virtually every color combination and style, so it is great for beginners. Embellished with embroidery, the flowers take on a life of their own. The fussy-cut quilt remains one of my favorites and went on to become the center of *Palampore Tree of Life* (page 109). It uses a fabric that I bought in Paris years ago.

French fabric used for fussy-cut flowers

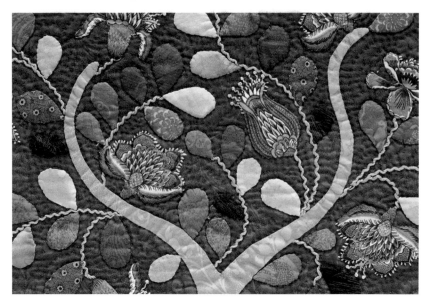

Fussy-cut flowers

Materials and Cutting

¾ yard of fabric for background and borders

Cut:

1 square 16″ × 16″ for central panel; trim to 14½″ × 14½″ after appliquéing

12 pieces 2″ × 6″; subcut into 60 foundation triangles for inner border (pages 100–102)

4 squares 1½″ × 1½″ for inner border corners

2 strips 1½″ × 16½″ for outer border sides

2 strips 1½″ × 18½″ for outer border top and bottom

Fat quarter or ½ yard of fabric for tree

Scraps of fabrics for leaves, flowers, and border

Cut:

12 pieces 2″ × 6″; subcut into 56 foundation triangles (pages 100–102)

22″ × 22″ square of fabric for backing

22″ × 22″ square of batting

¼ yard of fabric for binding

Cut:

2 strips 1″ wide for 84″ continuous single-fold binding

Mylar heatproof template plastic

Freezer paper

Fabric-marking pencil and eraser

Foundation paper

Embroidery floss

Crystals, beads, or other embellishments

Construction

Refer to pages 7–11 for general appliqué information.

CENTER

1. Trace the design onto the background fabric.

2. Use Mylar and freezer paper templates to make the appliqués. Use a freezer paper template to position and cut out the tree. Clip the curves. Pay special attention to the center of the tree's "Y."

Position tree on the fabric's bias.

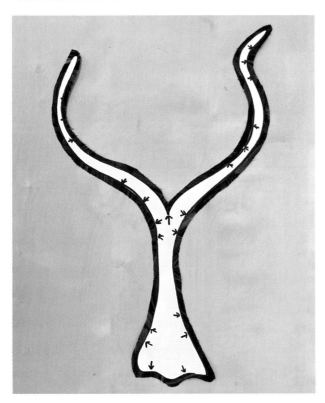

Cut out and clip curves. Arrows show where I have clipped the curves.

3. Remove the freezer paper tree and baste through the center of the trunk, matching the fabric to the tree outline.

Baste tree to background.

4. Embroider all small branch stems, using 6 strands of floss. Then add the appliqué and embroidery as directed for the individual flowers in Part 1: The Flowers (pages 12–51).

5. Erase any pencil lines and press carefully. Trim to 14½″ × 14½″.

BORDERS

1. Prepare 4 foundation inner border strips for a finished size of 1˝ × 14˝ (pages 100–102). Starting and finishing with the background-colored triangles, make the foundation-pieced strips and trim to 1½˝ × 14½˝.

2. With colored triangles pointing away from the center, sew 2 strips to the top and bottom of the appliquéd center square using a ¼˝ seam allowance. Press seam allowances toward the center.

3. Sew a 1½˝ × 1½˝ square to each end of the remaining 2 strips. Press the seam allowances toward the squares. Sew the strips to the sides. Press the seam allowances toward the triangles.

4. Sew a 1½˝ × 16½˝ strip of background fabric to the top and bottom. Press seam allowances toward the outer borders.

5. Sew the 1½˝ × 18½˝ strips to the sides. Press the seam allowances toward the borders.

6. Remove the paper from the foundation strips. Appliqué the corner motifs, if desired. Press.

FINISHING

1. Layer the quilt top with batting and backing. Quilt as desired. I echo quilted throughout the center square and outline quilted the foundation triangles. Trim the quilt to 18½˝ × 18½˝.

2. Stitch the binding strips together to form one long strip. Fold under ¼˝ at one end of the binding strip. Starting in the center of one side, sew the binding all around the quilt using a ¼˝ seam allowance. Overlap the ends of the binding ½˝ and trim. Fold over ¼˝ along the raw edge and blindstitch to the back.

Enlarge the pattern by 400% to trace the full-size design on the background fabric.

Pillow Option

Use the central tree pattern shown, without borders. Center it on fabric cut to 16″ × 16″ or larger for your desired pillow size. Trim to 15½″ × 15½″ after appliqué. Follow the Finishing instructions (page 68) to complete the pillow.

This silk pillow uses highly contrasting pinks and Swarovski crystals in the flower centers.

Flowers with crystal centers

Jacobean Tree of Life pillow, 15½″ × 15½″

STAR FLOWER HEART
WALLHANGING

26″ × 26″ quilt top

16″ × 16″ center block

This quilt uses a 16″ Star Flower block (page 76) with the Fuchsia Border and Corner Design (page 104). It was appliquéd as one piece without seams. Any of the 16″ blocks from the earlier projects in this chapter could be substituted for the central block with equal success.

Alternate Easy Template Flowers (page 47)

Alternate Michaelmas Daisy (pages 30–31)

Alternate Mimosa / Floral Spray / Berries (pages 32–33)

Alternate Single Fuchsia (page 104)

Star Flower (pages 39–40)

Materials and Cutting

1¾ yards of purple fabric for background, backing, and binding

Cut:

1 square 27″ × 27″; trim to 26″ × 26″ after appliquéing

1 square 30″ × 30″ for backing

3 strips 1″ wide for 114″ continuous single-fold binding

1 fat quarter or ½ yard of fabric for stems

Cut:

⅜″-wide bias strips, as needed (*Refer to page 53 for cutting bias strips.*)

Use remainder for leaves.

⅛ yard each of deep mauve, light mauve, fuchsia pink, pale pink, orange, and butter yellow fabrics for appliqué

Scrap of fabric for fussy cutting flower centers

30″ × 30″ square of batting

Stem green, fuchsia pink, and butter yellow embroidery floss

Mylar heatproof template plastic

Freezer paper

Construction

Refer to pages 7–11 for general appliqué information.

APPLIQUÉ

1. Fold the 27″ × 27″ square in half horizontally and vertically; press to mark the center. Trace the heart design onto the fabric, matching the centers. Mark the 16″ block lines. Place the corner design (page 104) on the 16″ lines as shown and trace. Repeat for all 4 corners.

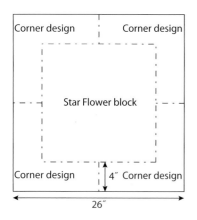

Star Flower Heart layout

2. Use Mylar and freezer paper templates to make the appliqués.

3. Appliqué or embroider all the stems. Then add the appliqué and embroidery as directed for the individual flowers in Part 1: The Flowers (pages 12–51).

4. Erase all pencil lines and press carefully with a hot iron. Trim to 26″ × 26″.

FINISHING

1. Layer with batting and backing; baste the layers together. Quilt as desired. I chose to echo quilt closely throughout. Press lightly and square up the piece.

2. Stitch the binding strips together into one long strip. Fold under ¼″ at one end of the binding strip. Starting in the center of one side, sew the binding around the quilt, using a ¼″ seam allowance. Overlap the ends by ½″ and trim. Fold over ¼″ along the raw edge and blindstitch to the back.

Refer to page 104 for the corner border design.

Enlarge the pattern by 400% to trace the full-size design in the center of the background fabric.

MEXICAN HEART
WALLHANGING

26½″ × 26½″ quilt top

16″ × 16″ center block

This 16″ block surrounded by a 3″-wide Simple Daisy and Hearts Border makes an attractive wall quilt.

Alternate Daisy (pages 20–21)

Alternate Easy Template Flowers (page 47)

Alternate Michaelmas Daisy (pages 30–31)

The Mexican Heart block would undoubtedly look lovely with the corner border design from *Star Flower Heart* (page 74). If desired, simply follow the layout instructions (page 76).

Materials and Cutting

1¾ yards of fabric for background, borders, backing, and binding

Cut:

1 square 30″ × 30″ for quilt backing

1 square 18″ × 18″ for center appliqué block; trim to 16½″ × 16½″ after appliquéing

2 strips 3½″ × 18½″ for border top and bottom

2 strips 3½″ × 24½″ for border sides

34 pieces 2″ × 6″; subcut into 168 triangles for foundation-pieced border (pages 100–102)

8 squares 1½″ × 1½″

3 strips 1″ wide for 116″ continuous single-fold binding

⅛ yard each of purple, deep turquoise, sunshine yellow, pale pink, and ecru fabrics for appliqué and foundation triangles

Cut:

7 strips 2″ × 6″ each of the above 5 colors; subcut into 160 triangles (32 from each color) for foundation-pieced border (pages 100–102). Use remainder for flowers.

12″ × 12″ each of 3 values of green fabric for leaves and stems

Cut:

⅜″-wide bias strips, as needed

Use remainder for leaves.

Fabric for fussy cutting flowers

30″ × 30″ square of batting

Bright green embroidery floss

Construction

Refer to pages 7–11 for general appliqué information.

CENTER

1. Trace the design onto the background fabric for the center block.

2. Use Mylar and freezer paper templates to make the appliqués.

3. Appliqué or embroider all the stems. Then add the appliqué and embroidery as directed for the individual flowers in Part 1: The Flowers (pages 12–51).

4. Erase all pencil lines and press carefully with a hot iron. Trim to 16½˝ × 16½˝.

BORDERS

1. Prepare 4 foundation strips for a finished size of 1˝ × 16˝ (page 100–102). Starting and finishing with background-colored triangles, make the foundation-pieced strips and trim to 1½˝ × 16½˝.

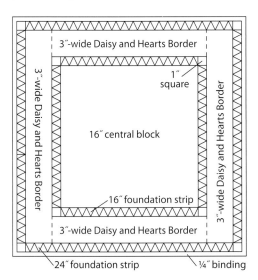

Mexican Heart layout

2. With colored triangles pointing away from the center, sew 2 of the foundation-pieced strips to the top and bottom of the central square, using a ¼˝ seam allowance. Press the seam allowances toward the center.

3. Sew a 1½˝ × 1½˝ background-colored square to each end of the remaining 2 foundation-pieced strips. Press the seam allowances toward the squares.

4. Sew the remaining strips to the sides. Press the seam allowances toward the triangles.

5. Sew 3½˝ × 18½˝ strips to the top and bottom, pressing the seam allowances toward the inner border. Sew 3½˝ × 24½˝ strips to the sides. Press toward the inner border. Remove the paper from the inner border foundation strips.

> **TIP**
>
> *The appliqué border will distort less if you attach all borders to the quilt top before you appliqué the hearts and flowers.*

6. Prepare 4 foundation strips for a finished size of 1˝ × 24˝ (page 100–102). Starting and finishing with background-colored triangles, make the foundation-pieced strips and trim to 1½˝ × 24½˝.

7. With colored triangles pointing toward the center, sew the 2 strips to the top and bottom of the central square, using a ¼˝ seam allowance. Press the seam allowance toward the center.

8. Sew a 1½˝ × 1½˝ background-colored square to each end of the remaining 2 strips. Press the seam allowance toward the squares.

9. Sew the remaining strips to the sides. Press the seam allowance toward the triangles.

> **TIP**
>
> *It is best to stabilize the outermost foundation border with the binding before quilting. Do not remove the paper until all appliqué is completed. The foundation triangles are still fragile and can easily pull and fray during the appliqué of the hearts and flowers; the binding adds the stability needed.*

10. Stitch the binding strips together into one long strip. Fold under ¼˝ at one end of the binding strip. Starting in the center of one side, sew the binding all the way around the quilt top, using a ¼˝ seam allowance. Overlap the ends by ½˝ and trim.

11. Use the Simple Daisy and Hearts Border template (page 103); align it with a 3″ border and trace the design. You only need to mark the center circle for the daisies and the heart outline for the hearts.

12. Appliqué and embroider the hearts and daisies. Appliqué the circles in the foundation strip corners using the daisy center template from *Mexican Heart* (below).

> ■ **NOTE**
>
> *Fussy-cut circles would add pizzazz if you have any suitable fabric.*

13. Erase all pencil lines and press carefully with a hot iron.

14. Remove all paper from the outer border foundation triangle strips. Press well.

FINISHING

1. Layer with batting and backing; quilt as desired. I heavily echo quilted the center block heart and the 3″ borders; I outlined the triangles in the foundation borders. Stabilize the outermost edge of batting and backing by quilting along the base of the triangles right next to the binding.

2. Trim the backing and batting even with the quilt top.

3. Attach the binding, and then fold over ¼″ along the raw edge of the binding and blindstitch to the back.

Mexican Heart pillow. With some wild fabric, even wilder fussy cutting, and a little adaptation, I made a variation of this pillow for my son. I enlarged the central heart to a finished 17″ square for a final pillow of 21½″ × 21½″. To do so, I used 4 foundation strips with an unfinished size of 1½″ × 17½″. For the plain outer borders, I used 2 strips 1½″ × 19½″ and 2 strips 1½″ × 21½″.

Enlarge the pattern by 400% to trace the full-size design on the background fabric.

VINE FRUITS
TABLE RUNNER

10½″ × 40½″ quilt

This design has improved since my earlier version (page 84). With a few subtle changes, it has now become a little more elegant. I also used this design in the center of *Jacobean Sampler* (page 91).

Grapes / Wisteria / Hanging Blooms (page 25)

Alternate Mimosa / Floral Spray / Berries (pages 32–33)

Pomegranate (pages 37–38)

Single Fuchsia (pages 23–24)

Materials and Cutting

1¼ yards of fabric for background, borders, backing, and binding

Cut:

1 piece 10˝ × 40˝; trim to 8½˝ × 38½˝ after appliquéing

1 piece 14˝ × 44˝ for backing

20 pieces 2˝ × 6˝; subcut into 96 triangles for foundation-pieced border (pages 100–102)

4 squares 1½˝ × 1½˝

3 strips 1˝ wide for 112˝ continuous single-fold binding

10˝ × 10˝ square of fabric for stems and leaves

Cut:

⅜˝-wide bias strips, as needed *(Refer to page 53 for cutting bias strips.)*

Use remainder for leaves.

12˝ × 12˝ square each of soft red, gold, lilac, deep red, and deep turquoise fabrics for appliqués and foundation triangles

Cut:

4 pieces 2˝ × 6˝ each of the above 5 colors; subcut into 92 triangles (19 from each color) for foundation-pieced border (pages 100–102)

12˝ × 12˝ square of darker green fabric for leaves

Scraps of 2 coordinating patterned fabrics for fussy cutting Pomegranate, inner petals of Fuchsia, and border corner decoration

Scrap of golden ochre fabric for inner circle of Pomegranates

14˝ × 44˝ piece of batting

Embroidery floss

Construction

Refer to pages 7–11 for general appliqué information.

CENTER

1. Trace the design onto the background fabric.

2. Use Mylar and freezer paper templates to make the appliqués.

3. Appliqué or embroider all the stems. Then add the appliqué and embroidery as directed for the individual flowers in Part 1: The Flowers (pages 12–51).

4. Erase all pencil lines and press carefully with a hot iron. Trim to 8½˝ × 38½˝.

BORDERS

1. Prepare 2 foundation strips with a finished size of 1˝ × 8˝ and 2 with a finished size of 1˝ × 38˝ (pages 100–102). Starting and finishing with background-colored triangles, make the foundation-pieced strips and trim to 1½˝ × 8½˝ and 1½˝ × 38½˝, respectively.

2. With colored triangles pointing toward the center, sew the 2 short strips to the top and bottom of the central rectangle, using a ¼˝ seam allowance. Press the seam allowance toward the center.

3. Sew a 1½˝ × 1½˝ background-colored square to each end of the remaining 2 strips. Press the seam allowances toward the squares.

4. Sew the remaining strips to the sides. Press the seam allowances toward the triangles.

> **TIP**
>
> *It is best to stabilize the foundation border with the binding before quilting. Do not remove the paper until all appliqué is completed. The foundation triangles are still fragile and can easily pull and fray during the quilting. The binding adds the stability needed.*

5. Stitch the binding strips together into one long strip. Fold under ¼˝ at one end of the binding strip. Starting in the center of one side, sew the binding all around the quilt top, using a ¼˝ seam allowance. Overlap the ends by ½˝ and trim.

6. Carefully remove the foundation paper. Press.

7. Appliqué a fussy-cut ¾˝ circle to each corner square. Press carefully.

FINISHING

1. Layer with batting and backing. Echo quilt the central panel and outline quilt the foundation triangles. Quilt carefully along the bottom edge of the triangles, up to the edge of the binding, to stabilize the batting and backing.

2. Trim the backing and batting even with the quilt top.

3. Fold the binding over ¼˝ along the raw edge and blindstitch to the back.

Enlarge the pattern by 400% and join along dashed lines. Trace the full-size design on the background fabric.

Original *Vine Fruits* design. When I first arrived in Canada and was suffering from the winter blues—or rather the winter whites of Quebec, when one becomes hungry and desperate for some color—I created the navy blue *Vine Fruits* as one of my earliest attempts at appliqué design.

FLORAL SAMPLER
WALLHANGING

28″ × 42½″ quilt (excluding prairie points)

This really is a sampler in the traditional sense of the word. It was crafted especially to document my flower designs created up to that point. A pretty piece in its own right, it has a faintly folkloric feel due to its ecru background and fussy-cut flowers. The prairie points are the perfect simple edging to a very busy quilt.

> **■ NOTE**
>
> *The construction of all the flowers is covered in Part 1: The Flowers (pages 12–51). The flowers are labeled on a full-size design for easy reference on the pattern pullout (pages P1 and P2).*

Materials and Cutting

3 yards of fabric for background and backing

Cut:

1 piece 30″ × 44″ for background; trim to 28½″ × 43″ after all appliquéing and embroidering

1 piece 32″ × 46″ for backing

Fat quarter or ½ yard of fabric for stems and leaves

Cut:

⅜″-wide bias strips, as needed for stems and vines *(Refer to page 53 for cutting bias strips.)*

1 fat quarter each of dark, medium, and light green fabric for leaves

1 fat quarter each of pink fabrics in 5 values, from pale pink to burgundy, for appliqués

1 fat quarter each of dark, medium, and light turquoise fabric for appliqués

1 fat quarter each of dark, medium, and light purple fabric for appliqués

1 fat quarter each of dark, medium, and light yellow fabric for appliqués

1 fat quarter each of dark, medium, and light blue fabric for appliqués

Variety of floral fabrics for fussy cutting

¼ yard of medium or coral red fabric, ⅛ yard of paler red fabric, and ⅛ yard of burgundy red fabric for flowers and prairie points

Cut:

60 squares 2″ × 2″ of medium or coral red for prairie points

30 squares 2″ × 2″ of light red for prairie points

30 squares 2″ × 2″ of burgundy red for prairie points

32″ × 46″ piece of batting

Stem green and 2 other greens, golden yellow, pink, orange, and other coordinating colors of embroidery floss for embellishment

Construction

Refer to pages 7–11 for general appliqué information.

CENTER

1. Trace the design onto the background fabric. (The design can be found on pattern pullout pages P1 and P2.)

2. Use Mylar and freezer paper templates to make the appliqués.

3. Appliqué or embroider all the stems. Then add the appliqué and embroidery as directed for the individual flowers in Part 1: The Flowers (pages 12–51).

4. Erase all pencil lines and press carefully with a hot iron. Trim to the desired size.

FINISHING

1. To form the prairie points, press each 2″ × 2″ square in half diagonally twice, right side out, to make a double-folded triangle. Repeat with the other squares until you have a total of 120 pressed triangles. (You can use a few more or less depending on your placement.)

2. Pin the triangles to the outer edge of the quilt top, with raw edges together and triangle points facing into the design. Insert each fold of the triangle into the pleat of the one before, so the overlap is approximately ¼″. Use 24 triangles on each short edge and 36 on each long edge.

Prairie point placement

3. Machine baste. Check that all prairie points are evenly spaced and that the corners match each other. Stitch through all layers with a ¼″ seam allowance. Press the prairie points outward and the seam allowance toward the quilt.

4. Layer with batting and backing. Echo quilt the central panel.

5. Trim the batting to just inside the pressed seam allowance of the prairie points. Trim the backing so it is a generous ¼″ larger than the completed quilt top on all sides. Fold under the backing edge and blindstitch to the prairie points.

INDIAN GARDEN
WALLHANGING

44½″ × 44½″ quilt

13″ × 13″ blocks

The strategically placed butterfly and extra tendrils make it difficult to recognize that the center of this quilt is actually made from four individual projects (pages 55–62) surrounded by three borders. The silk fabric and the abundance of crystals and beads immediately made me think of India—hence, its name. But this project would work equally well in cottons.

Materials and Cutting

2½ yards of fabric for background and binding

Cut:

4 squares 15″ × 15″; trim to 13½″ × 13½″ after appliqué

2 pieces 7½″ × 28½″

2 pieces 7½″ × 42½″

56 pieces 2″ × 6″; subcut into 280 triangles for foundation-pieced borders (pages 100–102)

8 squares 1½″ × 1½″

5 strips 1″ wide for 188″ continuous single-fold binding

½ yard of fabric for leaves, border dots, and stems

Cut:

⅜″-wide bias strips, as needed (*Refer to page 53 for cutting bias strips.*)

Use remainder for leaves and dots.

Fat quarters in 5 green fabrics from dark to light for appliqués

1 fat quarter of dark, medium, and light values of each of red, lilac, golden yellow, cream, beige, and turquoise fabrics (18 total) for appliqués and foundation triangles

Cut:

1 strip 2″ × 16″ from each of the above 18 colors, plus 2 additional strips selected from colors listed above; subcut into 272 triangles (14 from each strip) for foundation-pieced borders (pages 100–102)

3 yards of fabric for backing

Cut and piece:

Cut in half from selvage to selvage. Trim away selvages. Join with a central seam and trim to 48″ × 48″. Press open the central seam.

48″ × 48″ piece of batting

Stem green, dark gold, pale gold, turquoise, red, lilac, and beige embroidery floss

Large selection of colored crystals and seed pearls

> ### TIP
>
> *Stabilize the outermost foundation border with the binding before quilting. Do not remove the paper until all appliqué is completed. The foundation triangles are still fragile and can easily fray during the appliqué of the Chrysanthemum Border.*

Construction

Refer to pages 7–11 for general appliqué information.

CENTER

1. Trace the designs onto the background fabric.

I used *Butterfly and Berries* (pages 55–56), *Autumn Tiger Lily with Asters* (pages 57–58), *Forget-Me-Nots and Pansies* (pages 59–60), and *Baltimore Beauty and Bluebells* (pages 61–62) for the central panel. I chose the Simple Sawtooth with Circles Border (page 102) and the Chrysanthemum Border (page 105).

2. Use Mylar and freezer paper templates to make the appliqués.

3. Appliqué or embroider all the stems. Then add the appliqué and embroidery as directed for the individual flowers in Part 1: The Flowers (pages 12–51).

4. Erase all pencil lines and press carefully with a hot iron.

Corner circles template patterns

5. Trim each block to 13½˝ × 13½˝. Join the blocks together using a ¼˝ seam allowance. Press seams open.

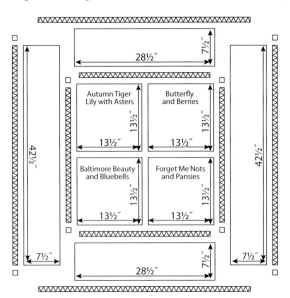

Assembly diagram

6. Referring to the pattern (below) for placement, add embroidered tendrils and appliquéd butterfly (shown in red) to tie the blocks together visually.

Add tendrils and butterfly.

BORDERS

1. Prepare 4 foundation strips for a finished size of 1˝ × 26˝ (pages 100–102). Starting and finishing with background-colored triangles, make the foundation-pieced strips and trim to 1½˝ × 26½˝. Sew a 1½˝ × 1½˝ square to each end of 2 of the strips. Press the seam allowances toward the squares.

2. Repeat to make 4 strips of 1½˝ × 42½˝ and sew a 1½˝ × 1½˝ square to each end of 2 of the strips.

3. With colored triangles pointing away from the center, sew the two 1½˝ × 26½˝ strips to the top and bottom of the central square. Press the seam allowance toward the center.

4. Sew the remaining shorter strips (with a 1½˝ square on each end) to the sides. Press the seam allowance toward the triangles.

5. Add the 7½˝ × 28½˝ strips to the top and bottom. Press the seam allowance toward the center. Add the 7½˝ × 42½˝ strips to the sides and press the seam allowances toward the center.

6. Repeat to join the remaining foundation strips.

7. Stitch the binding strips together into one long strip. Fold under ¼˝ at one end of the binding strip. Starting in the center of one side, sew the binding all around the quilt top, using a ¼˝ seam allowance. Overlap the ends by ½˝ and trim.

8. Press the entire quilt top, but leave the foundation paper in.

9. Transfer the Chrysanthemum Border design to the wide border.

10. Use Mylar and freezer paper templates to make the border appliqués.

11. Appliqué or embroider all the stems. Then add the appliqué and embroidery as directed for the individual flowers in Part 1: The Flowers (pages 12–51). Add the 268 green circles (template pattern B, page 89) and 24 turquoise corner circles (all template patterns, page 89).

12. Remove all foundation paper triangles; press.

FINISHING

1. Layer with batting and backing. Echo quilt the central panel and outline the foundation triangles. Quilt carefully along the bottom edge of the triangles up to the edge of binding to stabilize the batting and backing.

2. Trim the backing and batting even with the quilt top.

3. Fold the binding under ¼˝ along the raw edge and blindstitch to the back.

4. Embellish with crystals and beads as desired. I like to put beads on stamen heads. I also use crystals for Forget-Me-Not centers and where the Chrysanthemum petals meet the central circle (see the photo, page 105).

JACOBEAN SAMPLER
WALLHANGING

45½″ × 42½″ quilt

Combining five of the blocks used in earlier projects with a Simple 1″ Sawtooth Border results in a pleasing new take on a traditional Baltimore-style layout. Use one floral fabric for all fussy cutting to tie all the blocks together.

Materials and Cutting

2 yards of fabric for background and borders

Cut:

4 pieces 18″ × 20″; trim to 17″ × 19½″ after appliquéing

1 piece 9″ × 39″; trim to 8½″ × 38½″ after appliquéing

2 strips 1½″ × 45½″ for top and bottom outer borders

2 strips 1½″ × 40½″ for side outer borders

34 pieces 2″ × 6″; subcut into 166 triangles for foundation-pieced border (pages 100–102)

4 squares 1½″ × 1½″ for inner border corners

½ yard of fabric for stems

Cut:

⅜″-wide bias strips, as needed (*Refer to page 53 for cutting bias strips.*)

1 fat quarter each (or scraps) of light and medium green fabrics; 3 golden yellow fabrics in dark, medium, and light; ecru fabric; burgundy fabric; turquoise fabric; and lilac fabric for appliqués and foundation triangles

Cut:

4 pieces 2″ × 6″ each of the above 9 colors; subcut into 158 triangles (18 from each color) for foundation-pieced border (pages 100–102)

½ yard of coordinating floral fabric for fussy cutting

3 yards of fabric for backing

Cut and piece:

Cut in half from selvage to selvage. Trim away selvages. Join with a central seam, and trim to 49″ × 46″. Press seam open.

49″ × 46″ piece of batting

¼ yard of fabric for binding

Cut:

5 strips 1″ wide for 186″ continuous single-fold binding

Pale gold and ecru embroidery floss

Construction

Refer to pages 7–11 for general appliqué information.

CENTER

1. Trace the designs onto the background fabric. Designs should be centered vertically on the 18″ × 20″ background rectangles so there is a little extra space on the top and bottom of the block. Use the patterns for *Mexican Heart* (page 80), *Harvest Wreath* (page 68), *Spring Wreath* (page 65), and *Star Flower Heart* (page 76).

2. Use Mylar and freezer paper templates to make the appliqués.

3. Appliqué or embroider all the stems. Then add the appliqué and embroidery as directed for the individual flowers in Part 1: The Flowers (pages 12–51).

4. Erase all pencil lines and press carefully with a hot iron. Trim each panel to 17″ × 19½″.

5. Trace *Vine Fruits* (page 84) onto the 9″ × 39″ background piece.

6. Appliqué and embroider as in Step 3. Erase all pencil lines and press carefully with a hot iron. Trim to 8½″ × 38½″.

7. Join the blocks together using a ¼″ seam allowance and press the seams open.

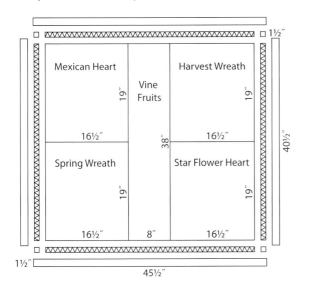

Assembly diagram

BORDERS

1. Prepare 2 foundation strips for a finished size of 1″ × 41″ and 2 strips for a finished size of 1″ × 38″ (pages 100–102). Starting and finishing with background-colored triangles, make the foundation-pieced strips and trim to 1½″ × 41½″ and 1½″ × 38½″, respectively.

2. Join a 1½″ × 1½″ square to each end of the 1½″ × 38½″ strips and press the seams toward the squares.

3. With colored triangles pointing away from the center, sew the 1½″ × 41½″ strips to the top and bottom of the quilt. Press the seam allowances toward the center. Sew the 1½″ × 38½″ strips to the sides. Press the seam allowances toward the center.

4. Sew the 1½″ × 40½″ background strips to the sides. Press the seam allowance away from the triangles. Sew the 1½″ × 45½″ background strips to the top and bottom. Press the seam allowances away from the triangles.

5. Stitch the binding strips together into one long strip. Fold under ¼″ at one end of the binding strip. Starting in the center of one side, sew the binding all around the quilt top, using a ¼″ seam allowance. Overlap the ends by ½″ and trim.

6. Carefully remove the foundation paper. Press.

7. Sew 4 corner motifs using 2 circles for each corner (the circles are made from template A, page 89). Press carefully.

FINISHING

1. Layer with batting and backing. Echo quilt the central panel and outer border. Outline quilt the foundation triangles.

2. Trim the backing and batting.

3. Fold the binding over ¼″ along the raw edge and blindstitch to the back.

FLORAL FANTASY
WALLHANGING

33½˝ × 68½˝ quilt

I made this quilt as a gift to my husband to celebrate our 25th wedding anniversary. Because I designed it as I went along, it developed a character all its own. I was thrilled with the quilt's joyful exuberance. It makes a gorgeous hanging and remains one of my most favorite quilts.

Materials and Cutting

2½ yards of fabric for background and binding

Cut:

1 piece 35″ × 70″; trim to 31½″ × 66½″ after appliqué

6 strips 1″ wide for 214″ continuous single-fold binding

41 pieces 2″ × 6″; subcut into 202 triangles for foundation-pieced border (pages 100–102)

4 squares 1½″ × 1½″

2⅛ yards of fabric for backing

Cut:

1 piece 37″ × 72″

½ yard of fabric for stems, sawtooth border circles, and leaves

Cut:

⅜″-wide bias strips, as needed (Refer to page 53 for cutting bias strips.)

Use remainder for leaves and circles.

1 fat quarter each of dark, medium, light, and very pale pink fabrics for appliqués and foundation triangles

1 fat quarter each (or scraps) of 2 dark, 2 medium, and 2 light golden yellow fabrics; 1 dark, 1 medium, and 1 light lilac fabric; 1 soft purple fabric; 1 soft white fabric; and 2 shades of cream fabric (for Stargazer Lilies) for appliqués and foundation triangles

Cut:

1 strip 2″ × 20″ of each of the above 13 colors; subcut into 221 triangles (17 from each strip) for foundation-pieced border (pages 100–102) (You will have a few triangles left over, but this excess will help you in your color placement.)

⅛ yard (or scraps) of dark, medium, and light fabrics for leaves

⅛ yard (or scraps) of floral fabrics for fussy cutting

37″ × 72″ piece of batting

Stem green, greens, stamen orange, and pale pink embroidery floss

Crystals, seed pearls, and beads

Construction

Refer to pages 7–11 for general appliqué information.

CENTER

1. Trace the design (pages 97–99) onto the background fabric.

2. Use Mylar and freezer paper templates to make the appliqués.

3. Appliqué or embroider all the stems. Then add the appliqué and embroidery as directed for the individual flowers in Part 1: The Flowers (pages 12–51).

4. Erase all pencil lines and press carefully with a hot iron. Trim to 31½″ × 66½″.

BORDERS

1. Prepare 2 foundation strips for a finished size of 1″ × 31″ and 2 with a finished size of 1″ × 66″ (pages 100–102). Starting and finishing with background-colored triangles, make the foundation-pieced strips and trim to 1½″ × 31½″ and 1½″ × 66½″, respectively.

2. With colored triangles pointing toward the center, sew the 2 short strips to the top and bottom of the central panel, using a ¼″ seam allowance. Press the seam allowances toward the center.

3. Sew a 1½″ × 1½″ background-colored square to each end of the remaining 2 strips. Press the seam allowance toward the squares.

4. Sew the remaining strips to the sides. Press the seam allowances toward the triangles.

> **TIP**
>
> *It is best to stabilize the foundation border with the binding before quilting. Do not remove the paper until all quilting is completed. The foundation triangles are still fragile and can easily pull and fray during quilting. The binding adds the stability needed.*

5. Stitch the binding strips together into one long strip. Fold under ¼″ at one end of the binding strip. Starting in the center of one side, sew the binding all around the quilt top, using a ¼″ seam allowance. Overlap the ends by ½″ and trim.

6. Appliqué circles to the points of all the colored triangles.

7. Carefully remove the foundation paper. Press.

8. Sew motifs in the corners if desired.

FINISHING

1. Layer with batting and backing. Echo quilt the central panel and outline quilt the foundation triangles. Carefully quilt along the bottom edge of the triangles up to the edge of the binding to stabilize the batting and backing.

2. Trim the backing and batting even with the quilt top.

3. Fold over ¼″ along the raw edge of the binding and blindstitch to the back.

4. Embellish with beads, crystals, and pearls.

Floral Fantasy Key

  A. Stargazer Lily

  B. Pomegranate

  C. Chrysanthemum

  D. Dahlia

  E. Daisy

  F. Double Fuchsia

  G. Michaelmas Daisy and Alternate

  H. Mimosa and Alternates

  I. Pansies

  J. Sunflower / Aster / Zinnia

  K. Daisy Alternate

  L. Easy Template Flower

Join to Panel 2.

Floral Fantasy—panel 1
Enlarge 300%.

Join to Panel 1.

Join to Panel 3.

Floral Fantasy—**panel 2**
Enlarge 300%.

Join to Panel 2.

Floral Fantasy—**panel 3**
Enlarge 300%.

Borders add such a nice finishing touch that I find them hard to resist. All the borders in this part can be used singly or in combination. *Palampore Tree of Life* (page 109) uses 7 of the borders to great effect. The same idea could be adapted successfully for any of the 16˝ blocks in the projects.

Simple 1˝ Sawtooth Border

This border is the simplest of all. It is adaptable for any size and is a perfect finishing touch for all of my designs. Although the general effect is scrappy, I am careful with the color choices and have found that the best borders for my designs only use the colors of the flowers themselves, and not the greens of the stems and leaves.

Once familiar with the technique, you can draw any size border to fit your projects.

1. Fold a piece of paper to make 4 layers with a minimum width of 15˝. Press and staple in place at the top and bottom. Draw 2 parallel lines 13˝ long and 1˝ apart. Mark triangles as shown. Each triangle should have a base of 1˝.

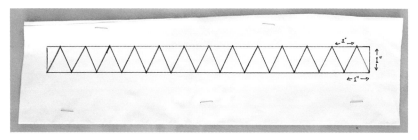

Draw parallel lines and add triangles.

2. Remove the thread from your sewing machine. Sew along all lines to needle punch all 4 layers.

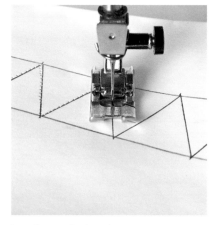

Needle punch along lines.

3. Remove the staples and cut into 4 duplicate copies of the foundation border.

4 identical copies of foundation border

4. I oversize my fabric triangles substantially for ease of placement during sewing. Cut 2″ strips; then cut into triangles with 2″ bases as shown. Cut the number of triangles specified in the project instructions.

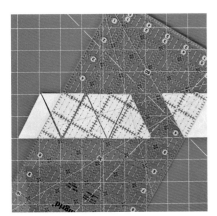

Cut triangles.

5. Organize your triangles into a color sequence, so that they are easy to reach when sewing.

6. Thread the machine with thread to match the background color. Starting with the background color, pin a triangle to the right side of the foundation piece so the right side of the triangle is facing up and the raw edge of the right side of the triangle overlaps the punched line by approximately ¼″. The left side of the triangle will overlap the straight edge of the foundation piece.

Placement of first triangle

7. Place a colored triangle on top of the background triangle, right sides together.

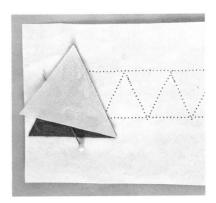

Place a colored triangle.

8. Holding the triangle in place, flip over the foundation paper and sew along the first diagonal line, starting ½″ before the beginning of the line and extending ½″ beyond the end.

Sew the first seam.

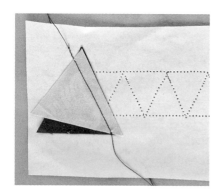

First sewn seam

9. Flip over the paper to the fabric side and finger-press the triangle open.

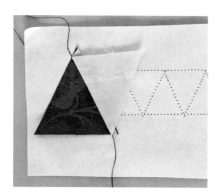

Finger-press open.

10. Place the next triangle over the second triangle, adjusting its position so the edge of the triangle covers the punched line by approximately ¼″. You may find that it helps to pin the triangle in place before you flip it over.

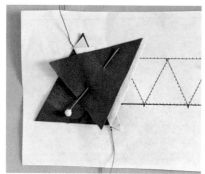

Pin in place.

11. Flip and sew as in Step 8.

12. Repeat Steps 7–11 until you have sewn the complete strip. Press with a hot iron.

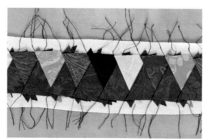

Sewn strip

13. Place the paper side up and trim all 4 sides ¼″ away from the perforated straight line to 1½″ × 13½″.

Trim the strip.

Trimmed strip

The strip is now ready to sew onto the center panel. Do not remove the paper at this point. You can use the perforated paper line for a perfect ¼″ seam allowance when sewing seams together. Remove the paper once the strips have been joined on all four sides or as specified in the pattern. To remove paper easily, pull and manipulate the strip gently; many of the paper triangles will simply tear away. Remove any remaining paper triangles manually, using tweezers for corners if necessary.

Simple Sawtooth with Circles Border

After the sawtooth borders are attached to the quilt top, sew circles at the points of the triangles.

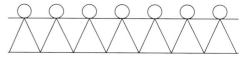

You may substitute ovals for the circles and further embellish with beads or crystals.

Simple Daisy and Hearts Border

Daisies and hearts alternate at 2″ intervals. The small oval drop at the end of the hearts provides added interest and is further embellished with an embroidered cross stitch. A tiny crystal would look good, too.

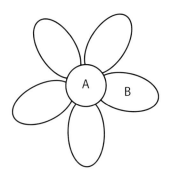

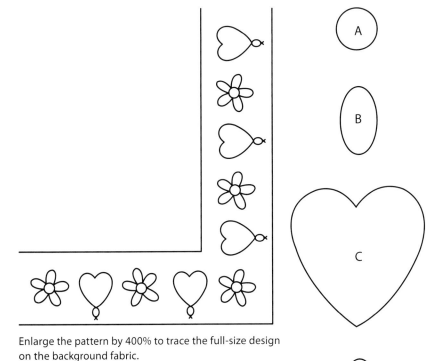

Enlarge the pattern by 400% to trace the full-size design on the background fabric.

TIP

For easier appliqué of the heart shape, cut the heart on the bias of the fabric. For smoother curves, clip the outer curves in several places as shown.

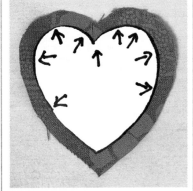

Clip outer curves to freezer paper in several places.

Fuchsia Border and Corner Design

Alternate Fuchsia
Enlarge placement diagram 200%.

Templates for Alternate Michaelmas Daisy are on page 31.

Repeat if extension required

Enlarge the pattern by 200% to trace the full-size design on the background fabric.

Chrysanthemum Border

This is one of my favorite borders. The structure of the flower means I can bring together many colors used in the quilt center. Chrysanthemums are a great excuse for some over-the-top embroidery and crystal embellishment. The 7″ width makes it adaptable to small wall quilts. It also has a clearly marked 10″ repeat, should you wish to lengthen the pattern. The pattern is given for one full side of *Indian Garden* (page 88), including corner turns. Join borders A and B for one complete side, including corner turns.

Chrysanthemum Border A

Enlarge the pattern by 400% to trace the full-size design on the background fabric.

10″ repeat

Chrysanthemum Border B

Enlarge the pattern by 400% to trace the full-size design on the background fabric.

The templates for the Chrysanthemum flower used in this border are on page 17.

GALLERY

Trellis of Red Flowers, 70″ × 77″

September Garden, 62″ × 62″

Summer Rhapsody, 62″ × 62″

Palampore Tree of Life, 50½″ × 50½″

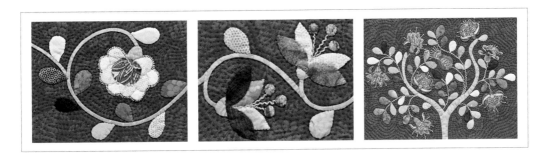

Spring Revival, 34″ × 60″

Photo by Nina Camacho

About the Author

Deborah Kemball moved to Montreal, Quebec, in Canada, in 2005. The influence of Montreal's long white winters changed her quilting style for good—from white wholecloth quilts to those that are a riot of color and tangled vines and flowers.

After graduating from university as a pharmacologist and physiologist in 1981, she left the United Kingdom with her husband to travel extensively with his job. She has lived in Holland, Cyprus, Costa Rica, Venezuela, and Canada, and each country has had its own influence on her work. She did not have many quilting resources, so she taught herself to quilt from a minimum of books, all before the advent of the Internet. As a completely self-taught quilter, she has developed her very own individual style. Her biggest creative influence comes from her love of the European cottons, silks, and chintzes of the eighteenth and nineteenth centuries, which were themselves inspired by Indian designs.

As a mother of four sons, she says that she would have achieved little without their help and nothing at all without the support of her husband, who has been her greatest source of encouragement. Furthermore, she is both amazed and hugely grateful that the entire family has happily tolerated, without complaint, more than sixteen years of being covered in stray threads and pricked by needles left in surprising places.

Great Titles *from* C&T PUBLISHING

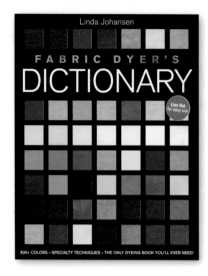

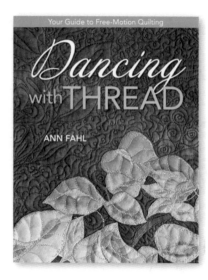

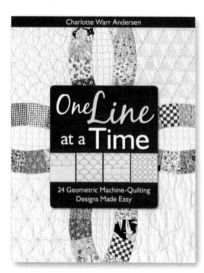

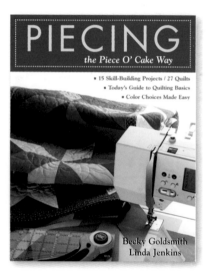

Available at your local retailer or **www.ctpub.com** *or* **800-284-1114**

For a list of other fine books from C&T Publishing, visit our website to view our catalog online

C&T PUBLISHING, INC.
P.O. Box 1456
Lafayette, CA 94549
800-284-1114

Email: ctinfo@ctpub.com
Website: www.ctpub.com

C&T Publishing's professional photography services are now available to the public. Visit us at www.ctmediaservices.com.

Tips and Techniques can be found at www.ctpub.com > Consumer

For quilting supplies:

COTTON PATCH
1025 Brown Ave.
Lafayette, CA 94549
Store: 925-284-1177
Mail order: 925-283-7883

Email: CottonPa@aol.com
Website: www.quiltusa.com

Note: Fabrics used in the quilts shown may not be currently available, as fabric manufacturers keep most fabrics in print for only a short time.